D1287575

SHERRILYN KENYON'S

Lords of Avalon

SWORD of DARKNESS

RDS OF AVALON: SWORD OF DARKNESS. Contains material originally published in magazine form as LORDS OF AVALON: SWORD OF DARKNESS #1-6. First printing 2008. ISBN# 978-0-7851-2766-6. Published MARVEL PUBLISHING, INC., a subsidiary of MARVEL ENTERTAINMENT, INC. OFFICE OF PUBLICATION: 417 5th Avenue, New York, NY 10016. $19.99 per py in the U.S. and $21.00 in Canada (GST #R127032852); Canadian Agreement #40668537. **Printed in Canada**. ALAN FINE, CEO Marvel Toys & Publishing Divisions and CMO Marvel Characters, Inc.; DAVID GABRIEL, SVP of Publishing Sales & rculation; DAVID BOGART, SVP of Business Affairs & Talent Management; MICHAEL PASCIULLO, VP of Merchandising & Communications; JIM O'KEEFE, VP of Operations & Logistics; DAN CARR, Executive Director Publishing Technology; JUSTIN F. GABRIE, Director of Editorial Operations; SUSAN CRESPI, Editorial Operations Manager; OMAR OTIEKU, Production Manager; STAN LEE, Chairman Emeritus. For information garding advertising in Marvel Comics or on Marvel.com, please contact Mitch Dane, Advertising Director, at mdane@marvel.com. For Marvel subscription inquiries, please call 800-217-9158.

SHERRILYN KENYON'S

Lords of Avalon
SWORD *of* DARKNESS

Writer
SHERRILYN KENYON

Adaptation
ROBIN FURTH

Artist
TOMMY OHTSUKA

Letters
BILL TORTOLINI

Cover Art
TOMMY OHTSUKA WITH GURU EFX AND JUNE CHUNG

Assistant Editor
JORDAN D. WHITE

Editor
MARK PANICCIA

Collection Editor **CORY LEVINE**
Editorial Assistant **ALEX STARBUCK**
Assistant Editor **JOHN DENNING**
Editors, Special Projects **JENNIFER GRÜNWALD & MARK D. BEAZLEY**
Senior Editor, Special Projects **JEFF YOUNGQUIST**
Senior VP of Strategic Development —
Acquisitions & Licensing **RUWAN JAYATILLEKE**
Senior VP of Sales **DAVID GABRIEL**
Design **SPRING HOTELING**

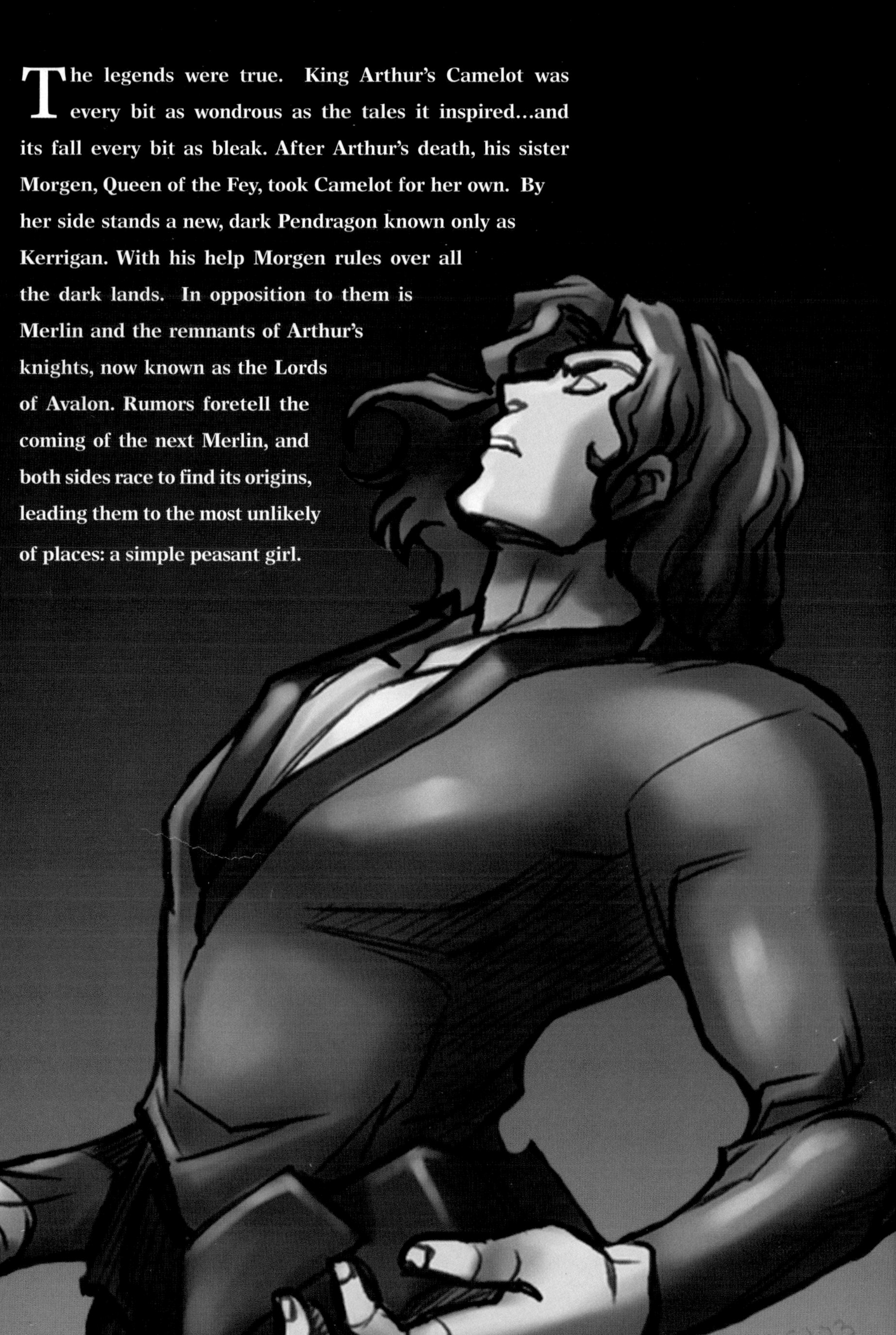

The legends were true. King Arthur's Camelot was every bit as wondrous as the tales it inspired...and its fall every bit as bleak. After Arthur's death, his sister Morgen, Queen of the Fey, took Camelot for her own. By her side stands a new, dark Pendragon known only as Kerrigan. With his help Morgen rules over all the dark lands. In opposition to them is Merlin and the remnants of Arthur's knights, now known as the Lords of Avalon. Rumors foretell the coming of the next Merlin, and both sides race to find its origins, leading them to the most unlikely of places: a simple peasant girl.

Long ago in a land that was lost in anarchy, there was an enchanted sword that had been forged by the hands of the Fey. For years it lay fallow in the dark forests of Britannia, waiting for the man destined to draw it.
Nurtured by the soul of the goddess Britannia and imbued with the magic of its makers...
The sword was said to grant immortality and superhuman strength to the one who wielded it.
Even the scabbard that held it was special. So long as a man wore it strapped to his hips, he would never bleed.
The sword could not be broken nor could it be defeated. Hence, there were many who feared both the weapon and the one who would someday lay claim to it.
For who could stop a man who wielded such a sword? Those who feared the blade sought to hide it. But in the end, even swords have destinies.

HE'S GONE THROUGH THE WOODS.
NAUGHT THERE BUT THE CLIFFS -- WE HAVE HIM NOW.
Embedded in a boulder and lulled by spells, the sword drowsed for centuries. But then one day a desperate young man happened upon it.
DAMN ME – MOVE!
HAH! NOWHERE TO RUN FOR YOU NOW, BOY.
AYE, TIME FOR JUSTICE TO HAVE AT YOU.
He was nothing remarkable – just a terrified young thief in need of a weapon to protect himself from those who would send him to the gallows.
GIVE IT UP, BOY!
YOU'RE BOUND FOR THE NOOSE FOR YOUR CRIMES. MURDERING WELP.
He had never been loved; he had never been wanted. Even his own mother had once tried to sell him to the highest bidder.
AAAAH!
THE BOY'S POSSESSED! RUN!
WHAT THE DEVIL--?
But where others saw a pauper and a scoundrel, the sword saw its master.
In that shivering young lad, the sword sensed power and a heritage that was not quite human.
Together, sword and man would bring all of humanity to its knees.
But the magical blade drawn on that fateful day was not the sword Excalibur...
YOU ARE MINE NOW...

...and this is not the tale of King Arthur.
HA HA!
AARRRGH!
YOU ARE THE ONE....
This is the story of Kerrigan, the champion of all things evil, and of his sword, Caliburn.

Many Years Later...

IT'S PERFECT. IT'S A MASTER-PIECE. IT'S--

--NOT GOOD ENOUGH.

NAY! IT CAN'T BE...
TAKE IT.
BUT I--

COME BACK TO US WHEN YOU'RE *WORTHY* OF THE TRADE.

HOW COULD THIS NOT BE WORTHY? 'TIS THE FINEST...
I *MUST* BE A JOURNEYWOMAN -- I *HAVE* TO BE! WITHOUT IT I AM NOTHING.

COME, CHILD.
I SPENT ALL MY TIME ON THIS... ALL MY PRECIOUS COIN. EVERYTHING.
I HAVE *NOTHING*, NOW.
'TIS NOT YOUR CLOTH THAT FAILED. THERE ARE TOO MANY WEAVERS HERE. THEY WILL ADMIT NO MORE UNTIL ONE LEAVES, OR DIES.

TAKE MY WORD FOR IT, CHILD. YOU ARE BETTER OFF WITHOUT BEING IN THE GUILD.
SHOULD THAT COMFORT *ME?*
HOW SO?
YOU HAVE MUCH LARGER CONCERNS THAN BEING AN APPRENTICE...

...BELIEVE ME.
WHAT?
KLAK!
HEY!

NO RECOGNITION. NO PAY FOR MY HARD WORK.
NO BUYER FOR MY CLOTH, NO LIFE OF MY OWN... I SHALL NEVER BE FREE.

WHAT GOOD ARE YOU?

EXCUSE ME, MISS?

IS THERE SOMETHING I CAN DO FOR YOU, MY LORD?
ARE YOU SEREN, THE WEAVER'S APPRENTICE?

WHY DO YOU ASK ME SUCH, MY LORD?
I AM GAWAIN, AND THIS IS MY BROTHER, AGRAVAIN.

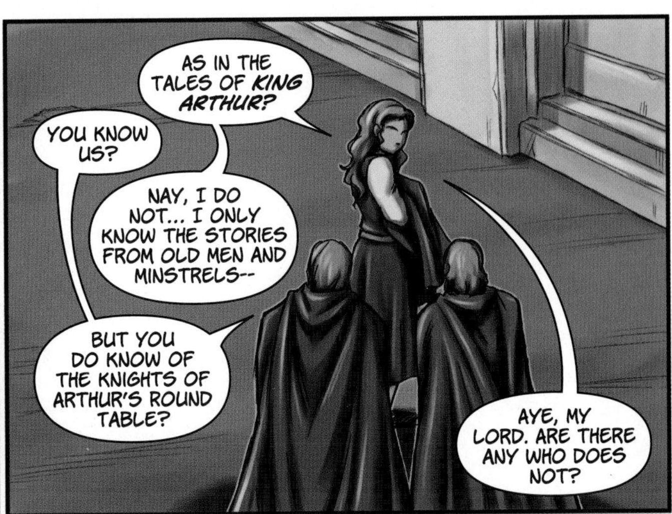
AS IN THE TALES OF KING ARTHUR?
YOU KNOW US?
NAY, I DO NOT... I ONLY KNOW THE STORIES FROM OLD MEN AND MINSTRELS--
BUT YOU DO KNOW OF THE KNIGHTS OF ARTHUR'S ROUND TABLE?
AYE, MY LORD. ARE THERE ANY WHO DOES NOT?

THEN YOU KNOW US. WE ARE THE SAME. MY BROTHER AND I WERE SENT TO FIND YOU. YOU'RE TO BE THE MOTHER OF THE NEXT MERLIN, AND YOU MUST COME WITH US SO WE CAN PROTECT YOU.
WHAT GAME IS THIS--?
'TIS NO GAME. YOU'RE TO COME WITH US. YOU'RE THE MOTHER OF THE NEXT MERLIN.

PLEASE, MY LORD. DO NOT ASK THIS OF ME... I AM A GOOD AND DECENT WOMAN!
WHAT--? NO, WAIT--
I HAVE NOTHING IN THIS WORLD BUT MY UNTARNISHED REPUTATION AND I BEG YOU NOT TO TAKE IT.
YOU'RE BLOWING IT, WAIN.

MY LADY, PLEASE. WE MEAN YOU NO HARM, WE ARE HERE TO PROTECT YOU.
PROTECT ME FROM WHAT, MY LORD?
MORGEN'S CLUTCHES. YOU BELONG WITH US, SEREN.
YOU'RE TO BE A BRIDE OF AVALON, AND YOU NEED TO COME WITH US BEFORE THE MODS FIND YOU, AND TAKE YOU TO CAMELOT.

MODS? WHAT THE DEVIL IS A MOD?
MINIONS OF DEATH. MODS. THEY WERE UNLEASHED BY THE CELTIC GOD BALOR BEFORE HE DIED, AND NOW MORGEN CONTROLS THEM.
SHE WILL SEND THEM AFTER YOU. MARK MY WORDS.

WAIT, SEREN!
MADMEN, BOTH!
OW!
DOWN THIS ALLEY, WAIN. I HEARD HER OVER THERE.
SEREN, COME BACK!
DON'T BE FOOLISH!
DAMMIT. WHERE IS SHE?
MERLIN WILL KILL US IF WE DON'T RETURN WITH HER.
I SWEAR, GAWAIN. I SHOULD'VE STRANGLED YOU AT BIRTH. OH, SURE, "WE'LL JUST TELL HER WHO WE ARE, AND SHE'LL COME WILLINGLY, NO PROBLEM."
SHOULD'VE LEFT YOUR RANK ASS IN THE TWENTIETH CENTURY.
YEAH? I WISH YOU HAD. I PREFER IT TO THIS.
WHAT WAS YOUR BRIGHT IDEA TO GET HER AWAY FROM MORGEN? HUH? YOU DIDN'T HAVE ONE AT ALL, DID YOU, BROTHER INTELLECT?
AHA! THERE SHE IS!

SEREN—
SEREN!
I CAN LOSE THEM IN THESE CROWDS!
HOW?
YOU CAN'T HIDE FROM US, SEREN.
NAY. I WON'T GO WITH YOU.
NAY, MY LORD, PLEASE LET ME GO.
SEREN!
WHHINNNNNY
ACCERO— ARE YOU TRYING TO KILL YOURSELF, WENCH?
MERCY, MY LORD, PLEASE!
FORGIVE ME MY RUDENESS, GOOD WOMAN. I HOPE I DIDN'T FRIGHTEN YOU OVERMUCH. IT WAS ONLY MY HORSE REARING THAT CAUSED ME TO SNAP.

AW, HELL...
HAVE YOU NEED OF ASSISTANCE, GOOD WOMAN?
AYE, MY LORD. I NEED TO ESCAPE FROM THEM.
THEN AS A KNIGHT AND A CHAMPION, I OFFER MY HUMBLE SERVICES TO YOU.
COME. I SHALL SEE YOU HOME WITHOUT HARM.
NAY!
DON'T LISTEN TO HIM, SEREN. RUN FROM HIM. NOW!
SEREN-- NO!
THANK YOU, MY LORD. YOU HAVE SAVED MY LIFE.
AND HOW IS IT I'VE SAVED YOUR LIFE?
THOSE MEN WHO WERE AFTER ME. THEY WERE MAD, OR MAYHAP DRUNK.
THEY CLAIMED I WAS TO BE THE MOTHER OF THE FABLED PHILOSOPHER, MERLIN. THANK THE LORD YOU CAME WHEN YOU DID. I SHUDDER TO THINK WHAT THEY WOULD HAVE DONE TO ME...
AYE. THERE WAS A HIGHER POWER THAT BROUGHT ME TO YOU THIS DAY.
OF THAT I HAVE NO DOUBT.

IT'S THEM! WHY WON'T THEY LET ME GO?
HAVE NO FEAR. I WON'T LET THEM TAKE YOU.

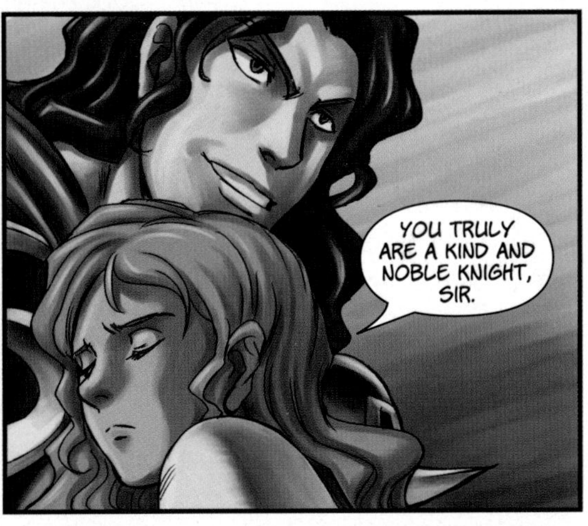
YOU TRULY ARE A KIND AND NOBLE KNIGHT, SIR.

I'M NOT TO LEAVE TOWN, SIR. MY MASTER WILL HAVE ME BEATEN FOR LEAVING WITHOUT HIS PERMISSION.
SHOULD WE RETURN, THEY WILL TAKE YOU. IS THAT WHAT YOU WANT?
NAY.
THEN HOLD TIGHT, UNTIL WE LOSE THEM.

ACCERO, ACCERO DOMINI DOYAN!
GOD IN HEAVEN!

SKKREECH!
BLOODY FLIPPIN' HELL!
BASTARDS!

WHAT IS THIS? WHAT ARE YOU?
YOU'RE LOST IN A DREAM.

SLEEP, LITTLE ONE.

SLEEP...

SLEEP.

SHE IS *OURS* AND THERE'S NOTHING YOU CAN DO.

EAT FIRE, YOU BASTARD.

WELCOME BACK, MY LORD.

GIVE HIM EXTRA OATS.
AYE, MY LORD.

STUPID MOUSE.

TRUSTING LITTLE FOOL.
YOU REACHED OUT FOR HELP AND NOW YOU ARE DAMNED FOR IT. THINK YOU THAT CLOTH WILL PROTECT YOU FROM ANYTHING? LEAST OF ALL, ME?

WHAT DO YOU WANT, SHAROC?
MISTRESS MORGEN WANTS WORD WITH YOU, MY LORD.
TELL HER I WILL COME IN MY OWN GOOD TIME.

I... SEE.

LEAVE ME, OR DIE!
YES, MY LORD.

ANIR.
AYE, MY LORD?
GUARD HER AND LET ME KNOW THE INSTANT SHE WAKES.
AYE, MY LORD.
Elsewhere...
UNBELIEVABLE...
WHAT DO YOU MEAN, 'SHE GOT AWAY'?
LORD SMOOTH HERE TOLD HER SHE WAS GOING TO BE THE MOTHER OF THE NEXT MERLIN, SO SHE PANICKED AND RAN.
LET ME SEE IF I HAVE THIS RIGHT.
'GAWAIN, THE NOBLE AND CHIVALROUS KNIGHT OF ARTHUR. A KING'S CHAMPION, HIS PROWESS WITH WOMEN WAS UNSURPASSED.'

THAT *IS* YOU, IS IT NOT?
YES, AND ACCORDING TO THAT BOOK, ***YOU'RE*** AN OLD, BALD ***MAN***.

DO YOU WISH FOR DEATH?
I'M IMMORTAL, REMEMBER?

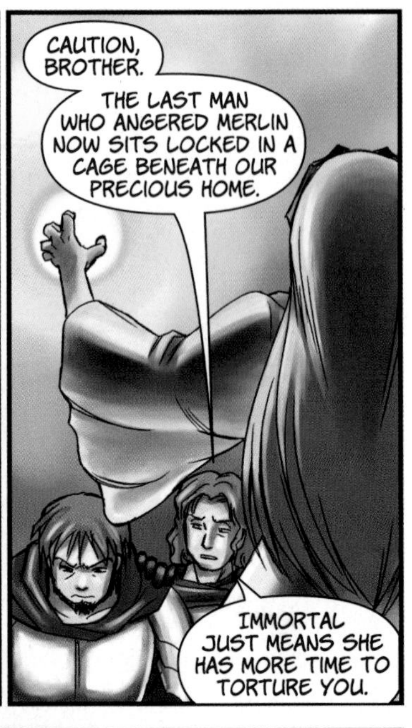
CAUTION, BROTHER.
THE LAST MAN WHO ANGERED MERLIN NOW SITS LOCKED IN A CAGE BENEATH OUR PRECIOUS HOME.
IMMORTAL JUST MEANS SHE HAS MORE TIME TO TORTURE YOU.

I'M SORRY, MERLIN.
BELIEVE ME, I AM NO LESS ANGRY OVER THIS THAN YOU. HOW DID KERRIGAN KNOW WHERE SHE WAS?

HE IS MORGAN LE FEY'S CHAMPION, AND HIS POWERS HAVE GROWN OVER THE CENTURIES. IF WE DO NOT STOP HIM SOON, HIS MAGIC WILL BE STRONGER THAN EVEN MINE. MAY THE GODS HELP US THEN.
I SHALL HAVE PERCIVAL RESEARCH HIM.
MAYBE THERE IS SOMETHING WRITTEN THAT EXPOSES A WEAKNESS, SOMETHING--

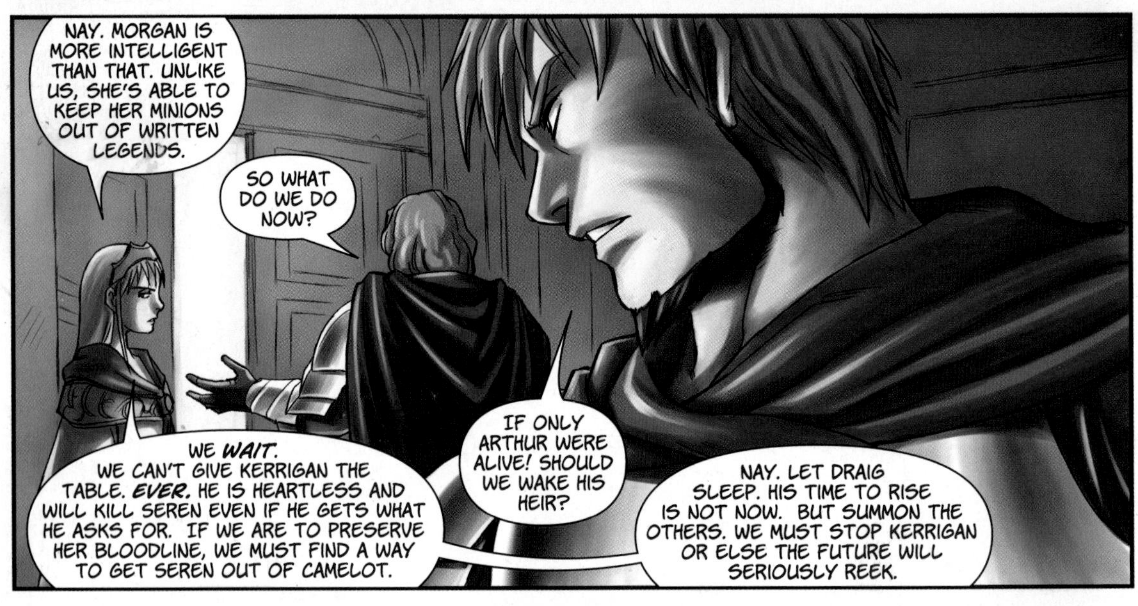
NAY. MORGAN IS MORE INTELLIGENT THAN THAT. UNLIKE US, SHE'S ABLE TO KEEP HER MINIONS OUT OF WRITTEN LEGENDS.
SO WHAT DO WE DO NOW?
WE ***WAIT***. WE CAN'T GIVE KERRIGAN THE TABLE. ***EVER.*** HE IS HEARTLESS AND WILL KILL SEREN EVEN IF HE GETS WHAT HE ASKS FOR. IF WE ARE TO PRESERVE HER BLOODLINE, WE MUST FIND A WAY TO GET SEREN OUT OF CAMELOT.
IF ONLY ARTHUR WERE ALIVE! SHOULD WE WAKE HIS HEIR?
NAY. LET DRAIG SLEEP. HIS TIME TO RISE IS NOT NOW. BUT SUMMON THE OTHERS. WE MUST STOP KERRIGAN OR ELSE THE FUTURE WILL SERIOUSLY REEK.

Meanwhile...

SO. YOU'VE FINALLY COME.

WHY DID YOU SEND FOR ME, MORGAN?

I WANT YOU TO KEEP A VERY CLOSE EYE ON OUR GUEST. IF I KNOW THAT BITCHTRESS, MERLIN, SHE WILL SET LOOSE ALL HER DOGS TO LIBERATE SEREN.

THEY DON'T SCARE ME. LET THEM COME. I COULD USE SOMETHING TO ALLEVIATE MY BOREDOM.

MMM.

NEITHER MERLIN NOR HER BASTARD MINIONS WILL EVER BREACH THESE WALLS.
WE'LL SEE.
WHY HAVE YOU STOPPED COMING TO MY BED, KERRIGAN?
I FIND YOUR BED TOO *CROWDED* FOR MY TASTES.
THERE WAS A TIME WHEN YOU DIDN'T MIND CROWDS. BUT YOU ARE VERY DARING, MY EVIL HEART. I'M NOT SURE WHY I ALLOW YOU TO SPEAK TO ME THUS.
THEN KILL ME, MORGAN.
WE BOTH KNOW I CAN'T, SO LONG AS YOU CARRY CALIBURN, AND ITS SCABBARD.

YOU HAVE BEEN WITH ME ALL THESE CENTURIES PAST, KERRIGAN.
ALWAYS SERVING MY... NEEDS. KILLING AND TORTURING OTHERS FOR MY WHIMS. YOU REMIND ME SO MUCH OF MY SON.
I'M NOT MORDRED.
NAY... YOU ARE NOT.
BE GONE FROM ME!
NOT THAT I WOULD EVER AIM TO PLEASE YOU, BUT AS YOU WISH, MORGEN.

In Kerrigan's Chambers...
OH, WHAT AN AWFUL DREAM...I SHALL HAVE TO TELL--

WHERE AM I?

FEAR NOT, HUMAN. I WON'T EAT YOUR HEART FROM YOU. NOT *YET*.

I'M DREAMING. I HAVE TO BE DREAMING.

NAY, NO DREAMS HERE, BOBBIN. ONLY ***NIGHTMARES***.

KERRIGAN, KERRIGAN – MY LORD DARKNESS, 'TIS TIME FOR YOUR RETURN.
NO!
LEAVE US.
YES, MY LORD.
WHAT ARE YOU?
EVIL INCARNATE.

IF YOU ARE EVIL, WHY DID YOU HELP ME?
I DIDN'T HELP YOU, LITTLE MOUSE. I ONLY HELPED *MYSELF.*

I DON'T UNDERSTAND. WHY AM I HERE? WHY IS THIS HAPPENING TO ME?
WHY NOT YOU? WHAT IS SO SPECIAL ABOUT YOU THAT YOU SHOULD BE *IMMUNE* FROM THE MACHINATIONS OF DAME FORTUNE?

I NEVER SAID I SHOULD BE IMMUNE TO ANYTHING. I ONLY WANT TO KNOW *WHY* THIS IS HAPPENING, AND *WHERE* I AM.
YOU ARE IN CAMELOT.

CAMELOT? BUT--
WHY THE SURPRISE, LITTLE MOUSE? CAN YOU NOT SEE THE BEAUTY OF IT? THE MAGIC?

THIS CAN'T BE...
OF COURSE IT CAN. THIS IS WHERE ARTHUR UNITED A KINGDOM AND SAW HIS WHOLE WORLD CRUMBLE, BEFORE HIS OWN NEPHEW BRUTALLY KILLED HIM AT CAMLANN.
ARE YOU ONE OF HIS KNIGHTS OF THE ROUND TABLE?

HA HA HA HA HA!
DO I LOOK LIKE SUCH?
NAY, WOMAN. I AM THEIR SCOURGE.
THEIR SCOURGE?
AYE. YOU RAN FROM YOUR BLESSED KNIGHTS OF THE ROUND TABLE WHEN THEY WOULD HAVE SAVED YOU.
SAVED ME FROM WHAT?
FROM ME.

Camelot
NO!

OH.

PLEASE, LET ME GO. I'M NOTHING SPECIAL -- ONLY A PEASANT, A WEAVER'S APPRENTICE.
AND I, TOO, WAS ONCE JUST A PEASANT -- A LIAR, A THIEF. I SPENT MY YOUTH RUNNING FROM THOSE WHO WOULD BEAT ME.
NOW I AM *KING OF CAMELOT.*
THE WHEEL OF FATE IS EVER ON THE MOVE, LITTLE MOUSE.
TODAY YOU ARE A SIMPLE APPRENTICE, BUT IN THE DAYS TO COME YOU ARE DESTINED TO MARRY AND BREED WITH ONE OF ARTHUR'S FAMED KNIGHTS.
THAT IS, IF ONE OF THEM IS MAN ENOUGH TO TAKE YOU.
HAVE YOU EVER TAKEN A MAN INTO YOUR BODY, LITTLE MOUSE?
AH!
YOU *ARE* A VIRGIN.
TELL ME, GIRL, HOW IS IT YOU'VE REMAINED SO CHASTE IN A WORLD OF HUNGRY MEN?
BY CHOICE, MY LORD! BY *MY* CHOICE!
AND I INTEND TO REMAIN A VIRGIN UNTIL THE DAY I *DO* MARRY.

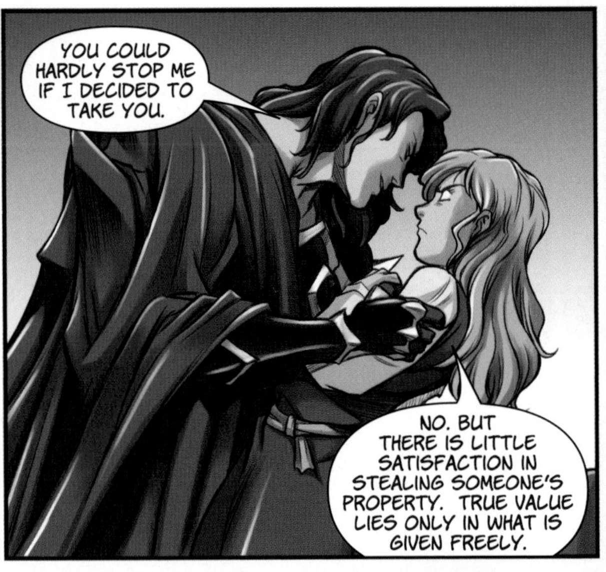
YOU COULD HARDLY STOP ME IF I DECIDED TO TAKE YOU.
NO. BUT THERE IS LITTLE SATISFACTION IN STEALING SOMEONE'S PROPERTY. TRUE VALUE LIES ONLY IN WHAT IS GIVEN FREELY.

WOULD YOU GIVE ME YOUR VIRGINITY IF I ASKED IT?
NAY!
THEN WHAT IS THE POINT OF ASKING WHEN THE ONLY WAY TO HAVE SOMETHING IS TO TAKE IT?

THEN I FEEL SORRY FOR YOU, MY LORD, THAT YOU HAVE SO LITTLE FAMILIARITY WITH COMPASSION.
TAKE MY HONOR IF YOU MUST, BUT KNOW THAT YOU STEAL THE ONLY GIFT THAT IS TRULY MINE TO GIVE.
AND KNOW THAT, DESPITE YOUR ARMOR AND YOUR SWORD...
YOU REMAIN A THIEF!

I'M NO THIEF! I AM KING!

WHAT IS YOUR NAME, GIRL?
SEREN.
IN MY LANGUAGE, LITTLE MOUSE, THAT NAME MEANS STAR.

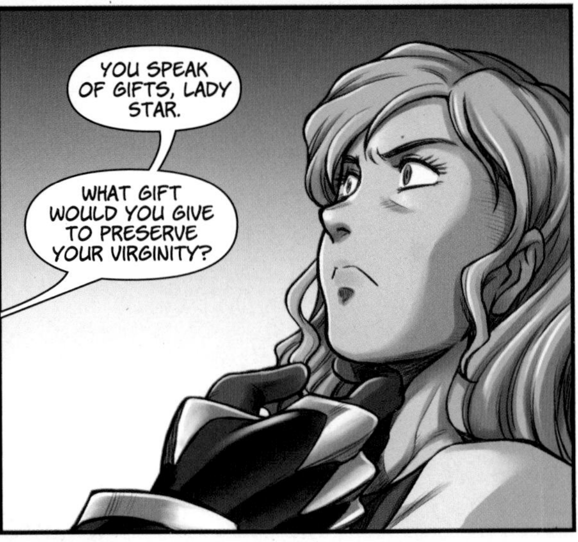
YOU SPEAK OF GIFTS, LADY STAR.
WHAT GIFT WOULD YOU GIVE TO PRESERVE YOUR VIRGINITY?

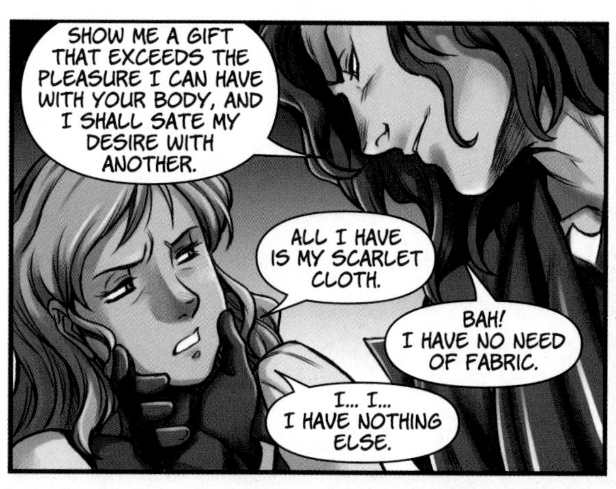
SHOW ME A GIFT THAT EXCEEDS THE PLEASURE I CAN HAVE WITH YOUR BODY, AND I SHALL SATE MY DESIRE WITH ANOTHER.
ALL I HAVE IS MY SCARLET CLOTH.
BAH! I HAVE NO NEED OF FABRIC.
I... I... I HAVE NOTHING ELSE.

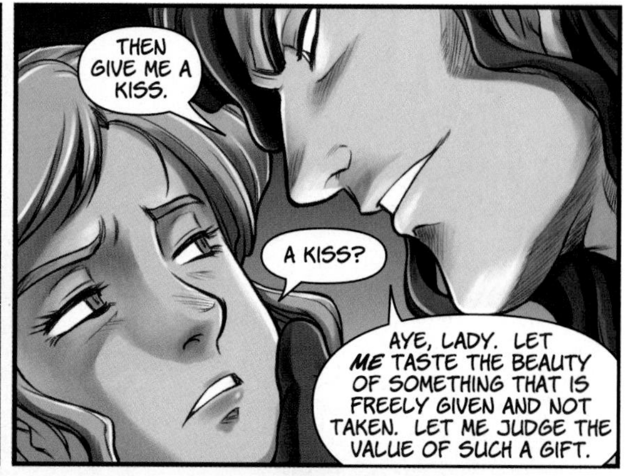
THEN GIVE ME A KISS.
A KISS?
AYE, LADY. LET *ME* TASTE THE BEAUTY OF SOMETHING THAT IS FREELY GIVEN AND NOT TAKEN. LET ME JUDGE THE VALUE OF SUCH A GIFT.

BUT I HAVE NEVER KISSED A MAN BEFORE!
A KISS OR YOUR BODY. WHAT'S IT TO BE?
HOW DO I KNOW THAT I CAN TRUST YOU?
YOU DON'T.
THEN I PRAY THAT YOU ARE A MAN OF YOUR WORD.

AYE, LADY. A KISS FREELY GIVEN IS MOST SWEET INDEED.

A PEASANT, YOU SAY...

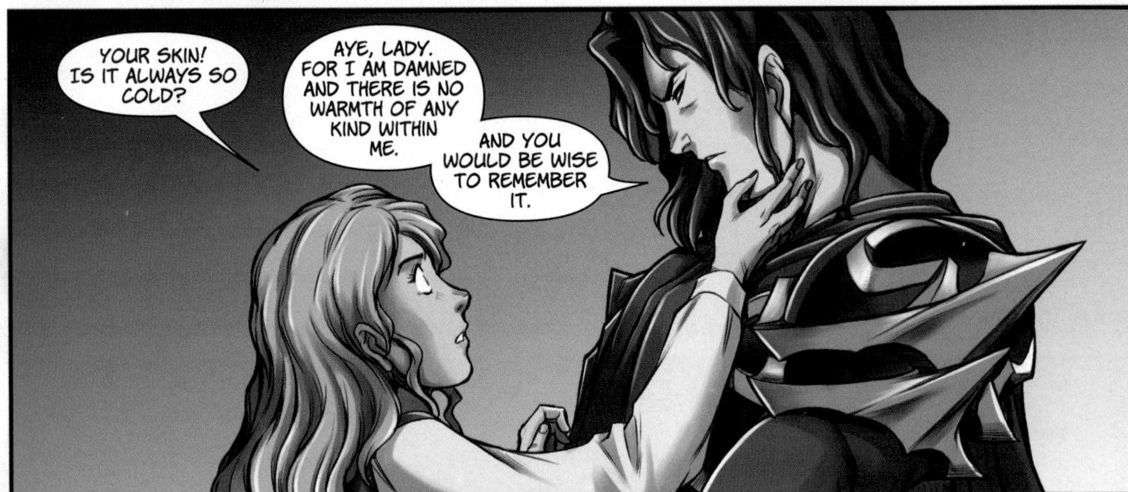

YOUR SKIN! IS IT ALWAYS SO COLD?
AYE, LADY. FOR I AM DAMNED AND THERE IS NO WARMTH OF ANY KIND WITHIN ME.
AND YOU WOULD BE WISE TO REMEMBER IT.

YOU MUST BE HUNGRY, LITTLE MOUSE. I SHALL HAVE FOOD PREPARED FOR YOU.

I COULD NEVER ABIDE A WOMAN IN RAGS.
MY DRESS!

Soon...

SO YOU ARE TO BE THE NEXT PENMERLIN'S MOTHER.
WHO ARE YOU?
THEY CALL ME MAGDA, AND I HAVE SERVED HERE SINCE BEFORE ARTHUR FELL.

I HAVE COME TO WARN YOU -- THERE ISN'T MUCH TIME! YOU MUST ESCAPE!
ESCAPE? FROM THIS FORTRESS?
AYE. THE KERRIGAN SAYS THAT HE WILL TRADE YOUR LIFE FOR ARTHUR'S ROUND TABLE, BUT HE HAS NO INTENTION OF KEEPING HIS PROMISE. AS SOON AS THE TABLE IS DELIVERED, HE WILL CUT OFF YOUR HEAD AND DRINK YOUR BLOOD!

THE KERRIGAN?
THE BLACK KNIGHT WHO BROUGHT YOU HERE. THE CHILD YOU ARE DESTINED TO CONCEIVE WILL THWART HIS AMBITION TO RULE THE WORLD OF MEN, SO HE WILL KILL YOU!

WHAT DO YOU PROPOSE I DO?
SEDUCE HIM AND WHILE HE DROWSES, STEAL HIS SWORD AND HIS AMULET. WITH THOSE YOU CAN ESCAPE.
AND WHAT WILL HAPPEN TO THE KNIGHT IF I TAKE HIS WEAPON AND HIS CHARM?

KNOCK KNOCK

MISTRESS SEREN, THE MASTER BIDS YOU JOIN HIM IN THE HALL.
REMEMBER, CHILD! REMEMBER WHAT I TOLD YOU!

AAHH!!

HA! HA! HA! GO ON, BOBBIN. LET IT FEEL YOU AGAIN!

DRYSTAN! YOU WILL NOT FRIGHTEN HER!
SMACK

THUD

OOOF

AAAH! FORGIVE YOUR SERVANT, GREAT KING!

PLEASE STOP! NO HARM WAS DONE TO ME.

IN SUCH CREATURES, MALICE ONLY GROWS. IF I LET HIM GET AWAY WITH THAT, HE WILL BECOME BOLDER AND MORE HARMFUL.
HE DIDN'T MEAN TO HARM ME.
IF YOU BELIEVE THAT, THEN YOU'RE A FOOL.
NAY, MY LORD. I'M NOT A FOOL.
I'M HUMAN, AND IT IS HUMAN TO FEEL PITY.

OUT OF MY SIGHT, WORM.
YES, MY KING.

THERE IS NO SPELL IN YOUR FOOD, MOUSE. YOU MAY EAT AND DRINK IN PEACE.

I'VE LOST MY APPETITE.

EAT!

IF I REFUSE, WILL YOU BEAT ME, TOO?

THE GRAYLINGS WOULD AS SOON SWALLOW YOUR HEART AS LOOK AT YOU. THE ONLY THINGS THEY RESPECT ARE CRUELTY AND POWER.
MIGHT DOES NOT MAKE RIGHT. AND POWER ALONE DOES NOT MAKE A KING.
WHAT RUBBISH DO YOU SPOUT, WENCH?

'TIS IN THE STORIES THE BARDS TELL OF THE KING OF CAMELOT. THE TRUE KING.
HE AND HIS KNIGHTS, WHO SAT AT THIS VERY TABLE, TURNED THEIR BACKS ON SUCH VIOLENCE. THEY PROTECTED THOSE WHO COULD NOT PROTECT THEMSELVES—

THERE ARE NO KNIGHTS HERE! ONLY DEMONS!
ARTHUR IS *DEAD*, BETRAYED BY THOSE HE LOVED, WHICH IS THE FATE OF ALL TRUSTING MEN!
THIS IS *NOT* ARTHUR'S TABLE, AND THIS IS *NOT* ARTHUR'S COURT. IT IS *LE CERCLE DU DAMNE* AND I AM ITS KING.
NOW EAT OR STARVE. IT'S ALL THE SAME TO ME.

WILL YOU NOT EAT WITH ME, SIR?
NAY.
ARE YOU NOT HUNGRY?
NAY.

DO YOU HAVE A NAME, SIR?
NAY, I DO NOT.
SURELY YOU DO. ALL MEN HAVE NAMES.

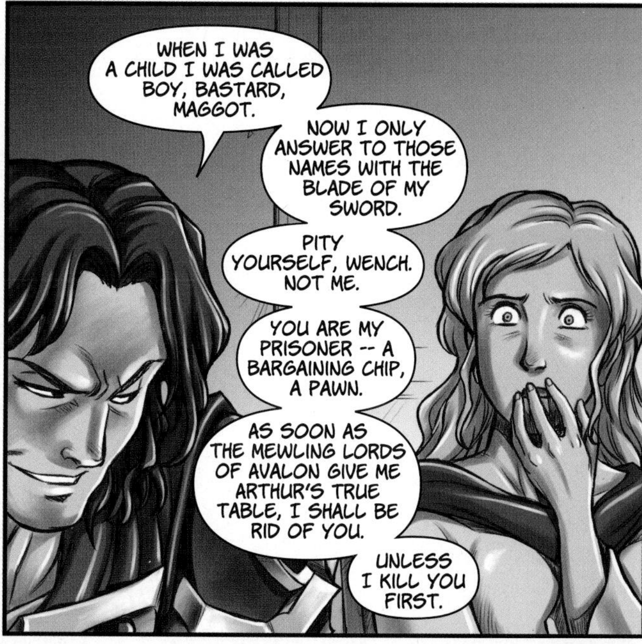
WHEN I WAS A CHILD I WAS CALLED BOY, BASTARD, MAGGOT.
NOW I ONLY ANSWER TO THOSE NAMES WITH THE BLADE OF MY SWORD.
PITY YOURSELF, WENCH. NOT ME.
YOU ARE MY PRISONER -- A BARGAINING CHIP, A PAWN.
AS SOON AS THE MEWLING LORDS OF AVALON GIVE ME ARTHUR'S TRUE TABLE, I SHALL BE RID OF YOU.
UNLESS I KILL YOU FIRST.

I DON'T BELIEVE YOU, SIR.
YOU WERE HUMAN ONCE, YOU HAVE TOLD ME SO YOURSELF.
SO FAR, IN YOUR WAY, YOU HAVE BEEN MERCIFUL TO ME.
BUT IF YOU WANT TO KILL ME, THEN KILL ME NOW AND END THIS GAME.

I RULE A KINGDOM OF VIPERS, LADY STAR, AND SOMETIMES I FORGET THAT I WAS ONCE A MAN. IT'S NOT A MEMORY I CHERISH, BUT IT'S ONE YOU REMIND ME OF TOO OFTEN.
I'M CALLED THE KERRIGAN. IT'S A FEY TITLE GIVEN TO ALL DARK MERLINS WHO COMMAND DEMONS. YOU MAY CALL ME BY THAT NAME.

WHY DO YOU WANT ARTHUR'S TABLE?
AT ITS HEART LIES A GREAT MAGIC, AND HE WHO WIELDS THAT MAGIC CAN RULE THE WORLD OF MEN.
BUT SURELY THE WORLD IS TOO BIG FOR ONE MAN TO RULE!
POWER HAS ITS PLEASURES, LADY MOUSE. AND YOU FORGET -- I'M NO LONGER A MAN.
NOW IT IS TIME FOR YOU TO RETURN TO YOUR ROOMS BEFORE YOU TRY MY PATIENCE ANY FURTHER.

ACCERO, ACCERO DOMINI...
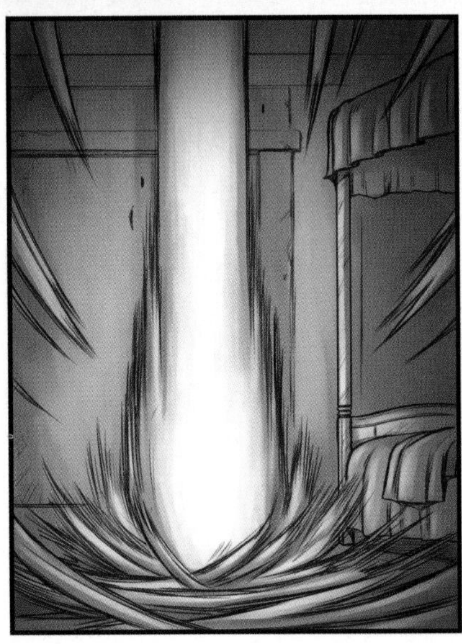

NO DOOR!

And soon, elsewhere...

WILL YOU NOT DRINK WITH ME, MY KING?

SPLASH

GRRRRR!

ATTACK AND YOU DIE. BEGONE! YOU BORE ME.

WHAT SAY YOU, MY LORD? ARE YOU ILL?
DON'T STAND BEHIND ME, BLAISE. NOT IF YOU WISH TO CONTINUE LIVING.

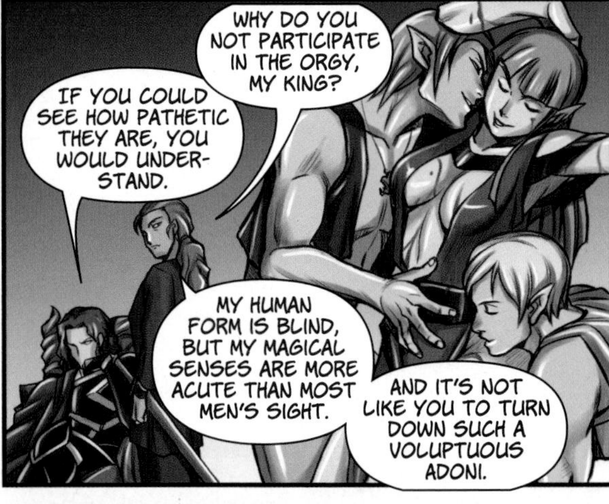
WHY DO YOU NOT PARTICIPATE IN THE ORGY, MY KING?
IF YOU COULD SEE HOW PATHETIC THEY ARE, YOU WOULD UNDER-STAND.
MY HUMAN FORM IS BLIND, BUT MY MAGICAL SENSES ARE MORE ACUTE THAN MOST MEN'S SIGHT.
AND IT'S NOT LIKE YOU TO TURN DOWN SUCH A VOLUPTUOUS ADONI.

AND IT'S NOT LIKE YOU TO STAND BY MY SIDE WHEN THERE ARE SO MANY WOMEN WILLING TO BE BEDDED.
I SENSED YOUR RESTLESSNESS. DO YOU WISH ME TO TAKE MY DRAGON FORM?
NAY. NOT EVEN FLYING WILL IMPROVE MY MOOD.

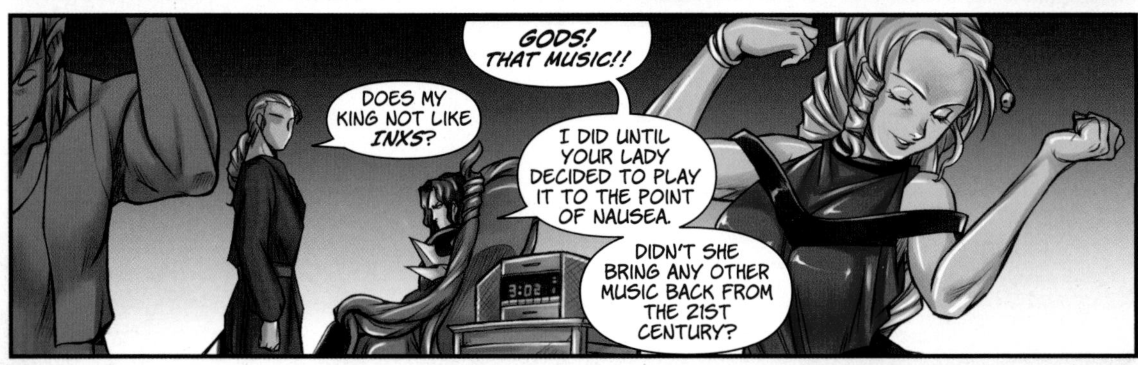
GODS! THAT MUSIC!!
DOES MY KING NOT LIKE INXS?
I DID UNTIL YOUR LADY DECIDED TO PLAY IT TO THE POINT OF NAUSEA.
DIDN'T SHE BRING ANY OTHER MUSIC BACK FROM THE 21ST CENTURY?
3:02

YOU ARE EITHER THE BRAVEST MAN EVER BORN, MY KING, OR THE MOST FOOLISH.
BOOF!

IT APPEARS OUR KING SUFFERS FROM A MALAISE.
WHAT DO YOU THINK WE SHOULD DO TO CHEER HIM?

YOU SHOULD BRING US HIS NEW PLAYMATE...
AYE, MY PET. I THINK THAT WOULD BE A WONDERFUL IDEA.

WHERE AM I?

LEAVE HER ALONE, MORGEN!

WHY SHOULD I? AS RULER OF THE FEY, I AM QUEEN HERE!
I'M QUEEN, AND YOU HAVE DISOBEYED ME!
NO ONE WEARS SUCH A COLOR IN MY WORLD. NO ONE BUT ME!

AND I *AM* THE LAW HERE, MORGEN. IT GOES WITH MY CROWN. THAT IS, UNLESS YOU WISH TO CHALLENGE ME FOR IT.
OUCH!
NO, MY EVIL HEART. IT IS *YOU* WHO ARE CHALLENGING *ME.*

YOU GAVE HER TO ME, MORGEN.
AND I PROTECT WHAT IS MINE, WHETHER IT BE MY THRONE, MY SWORD, OR MY PRISONER.
THAT'S FAR FROM COMFORTING.

AARGGH!

CAREFUL, MY LORD. REMEMBER WHO IT IS WHO GAVE YOUR POWER.
DAME FORTUNE IS FICKLE. ONE DAY A PEASANT, THE NEXT A KING, AND THE DAY AFTER, A PEASANT ONCE MORE.
ONE DAY A SORCERESS, THE NEXT A BAD MEMORY.

TOSTIG! DON YOUR ARMOR. KILL THE KING AND YOU SHALL REPLACE HIM!

I SHALL CHALLENGE HIM FOR YOU, MY LADY.
STAND DOWN, TOSTIG. I HAVE NO WISH TO THIN MY ARMY NEED-LESSLY.
BUT WHAT WILL HAPPEN IF HE KILLS KERRIGAN?
HE WON'T. TO CHALLENGE KERRIGAN IS TO COMMIT SUICIDE.

AAHHH!
BLAISE, GUARD THE GIRL!

AAAHH!

NO!

AH!
NO ONE MOVES UNLESS I SAY SO.

KERRIGAN IS INCREDIBLE, IS HE NOT?
WATCH HIM, SEREN.
LOOK HOW HIS MUSCLES STRAIN AS HE PARRIES.

LOOK AT THE POWER OF HIM. THE STRENGTH.

NONE SURPASS HIM IN SAVAGERY OR MERCILESSNESS.
IT MAKES YOU LUST FOR HIM, DOES IT NOT?

MORGEN! LEAVE HER BE!
AYE, MY CHAMPION! FOR NOW I SHALL.
BUT WILL YOU?

RETURN HER TO ME.

NO!

HA HA HA
HA HA HA HA HA
HA HA
HA HA

TAKE HER.

WHAT HAVE YOU DONE?
HUSH. YOU'RE SAFE NOW. MORGEN CANNOT HARM YOU HERE.
HOW CAN I BE SAFE WITH A DEMON LIKE YOU?

YOU MURDERED THAT KNIGHT!
YOU KNEW HE COULD NOT STAND AGAINST YOU, YET YOU FOUGHT HIM ANYWAY! FOR MORGEN'S AMUSEMENT!

...ACCERO, ACCERO DOMINI...

YOU ARE THE DEVIL!
AYE, LADY STAR. IT IS AS I TOLD YOU BEFORE.
YOU ARE IN HELL, AND I AM THE DEVIL WHO KEEPS YOU HERE.
YOU SHOULD HAVE GONE WITH GAWAIN WHEN YOU HAD THE CHANCE.
BUT BY YOUR OWN FREE WILL YOU CAME WITH ME.

SURELY THERE IS MERCY?
NAY, LADY. WE ARE ALL DAMNED BY OUR DEEDS, WHETHER THEY ARE THOUGHT OUT OR NOT.
NOW I SHALL LEAVE YOU SO THAT YOU MAY SLEEP.

KLAK
WHAT ARE YOU DOING, BLAISE?
SLEEPING. LIKE YOU I ANGERED MORGEN TONIGHT, AND I THOUGHT IT BEST I STAY HERE UNTIL HER IRE IS FOCUSED ON SOMEONE ELSE.
I WANT MY BALL, DRAGON.

YAWN

HOW LONG UNTIL WE REACH CAMELOT'S SHORES?
DO YOU THINK WE WILL BE IN TIME TO RESCUE SEREN?
THAT DEPENDS UPON THE WIND.

DREAM ON!

THUMP
AAAH! WATCH OUT!

NOW THAT WAS REAL MATURE.
DID I ASK YOUR OPINION?
NAY, BUT I FELT THE NEED TO GIVE IT.
AT LEAST THEY'LL LIVE. WHAT HAS POSSESSED YOU TO SUCH MERCY?
I CAN'T KILL THEM WHILE THEY'RE IN AVALON.
LIKELY STORY.

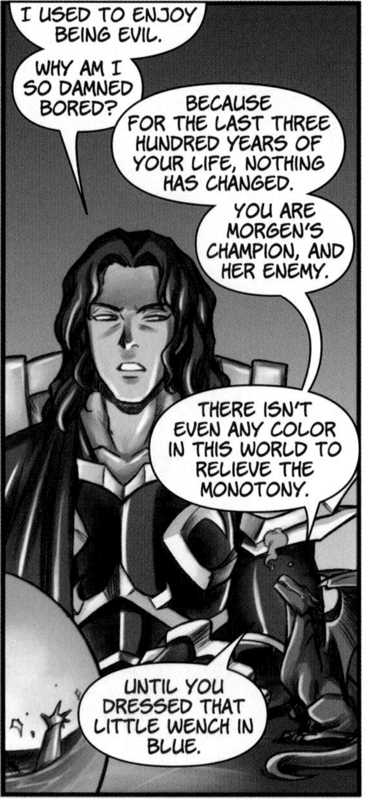
I USED TO ENJOY BEING EVIL.
WHY AM I SO DAMNED BORED?
BECAUSE FOR THE LAST THREE HUNDRED YEARS OF YOUR LIFE, NOTHING HAS CHANGED.
YOU ARE MORGEN'S CHAMPION, AND HER ENEMY.
THERE ISN'T EVEN ANY COLOR IN THIS WORLD TO RELIEVE THE MONOTONY.
UNTIL YOU DRESSED THAT LITTLE WENCH IN BLUE.

LEAVE HER OUT OF THIS.
IF ONLY *YOU* COULD, YOUR MOST ROYAL AND DUPLICITOUS HIGHNESS.

WHAT DO YOU MEAN BY THAT?
YOU'VE SEEN THE AURA AROUND HER. SHE'S NO MORE MORTAL THAN WE ARE.
THAT'S WHY SHE'S DESTINED TO BIRTH THE NEXT PENMERLIN. AND THAT'S WHY YOU WANT HER.

SHE'S A STUPID LITTLE PAWN AND NOTHING MORE.
IN MY DRAGON FORM, I'M FAR FROM BLIND. YOU *LIKE* HER, KERRIGAN.
SHUT YOUR MOUTH, MANDRAKE, OR I'LL MAKE YOUR SCALY HIDE INTO A PAIR OF BOOTS.

CRASSH
AAAHHH! HELP ME!

SEREN!

HELP ME!

HELP ME, KERRIGAN! HELP ME PLEASE!
HOLD ON, SEREN!
I'VE GOT YOU!
BRRRIIIPP
DAMN ME!
SEE YA, SUCKER! THIS MORSEL'S FOR THE MISTRESS!
BRING HER BACK, YOU BASTARD!

HEH, HEH, HEH!
OUCH!
WHOOSH
RELEASE HER!
NO! OH PLEASE DON'T! NOT HERE!
I CAN'T BREATHE... YOU'RE BREAKING MY RIBS!
WHOOSH

AAAHHH!

HELP!

BLESSED SAINTS, PROTECT ME!

OH!

YOU BEAST!
WHAT'S WRONG WITH YOU, WENCH? I JUST SAVED YOU!
YOU ALMOST KILLED ME! I WAS SAFER IN THAT MONSTER'S TALON THAN I WAS FREEFALLING THROUGH THE AIR!
SHE HAS A POINT, MY KING.
SHUT UP, BLAISE!
BLAISE WOULD NEVER DROP US.
SEE, THERE YOU GO AGAIN! YOU SHOULD BE KINDER TO THOSE WHO KEEP US FROM FALLING INTO THE SEA!
HOW DO YOU KNOW?
BECAUSE THE FALL WOULDN'T KILL MY KING.
IT WOULD ONLY MAKE HIM ANGRY.
AND THEN HE WOULD NAIL MY SCALY HIDE TO HIS WALL AS A TROPHY.
YOU HAVE NO CONSCIENCE AND NO DECENCY.
NOTHING IS PURE EVIL. THERE IS GOODNESS IN ALL.
I THINK SHE MISSED THE PART ABOUT YOU BEING PURE EVIL, MY LIEGE.
SHE HASN'T MET MORGEN, HAS SHE?
YOU KNOW... I'M THINKING MORGEN STILL WANTS THE GIRL.
OVER MY DEAD BODY.
MORE LIKELY IT WILL BE OVER MINE. THEY ALWAYS SACRIFICE THE DRAGON...

MORGEN! CALL BACK YOUR TROOPS OR LOSE THEM ALL!
GIVE ME THE PENMERLIN'S MOTHER!
NO!
ARE YOU SURE ABOUT THAT, MY LIEGE?
ABSOLUTELY. I'M BETTING YOUR HIDE ON IT.
TAKE KERRIGAN'S SWORD AND SCABBARD AND HE IS NAUGHT BUT A MORTAL MAN!
THE ONE TO BRING HIS HEAD TO ME WILL BE MY NEW CHAMPION!

WE'RE SCREWED, MY KING. ANY IDEAS?
WE'RE PULLING OUT OF CAMELOT!
ACCERO, ACCERO DOMINA...
KERBANG!
WHERE'D THEY GO?
DUNNO, BUT I SURE AS HELL AIN'T GONNA BREAK THE NEWS TO THE BITCH.

WHHOOSH!

THEY'LL BE COMING FOR US.
MORGEN KNOWS NOTHING OF THIS PLACE. I HAVE KEPT IT FROM HER FOR GOOD REASON.

OH... UM... THANK YOU!
PUT HER DOWN, BLAISE.

AND THE LORDS OF AVALON? THEY WANT SEREN, TOO.
THEY WON'T VENTURE HERE. THEY FEAR THIS CASTLE AND THE CURSE PLACED UPON IT.
THIS CASTLE IS CURSED?

AYE, LADY SEREN. WE'RE AT JOYOUS GARD.
THE HOME OF LANCELOT DU LAC?
THE SAME. WITH HIS FINAL BREATH, LANCELOT CURSED THE KNIGHTS OF THE ROUND TABLE. SHOULD ANY OF ARTHUR'S FOLLOWERS STEP FOOT IN THIS CASTLE, MISFORTUNE AND ILLNESS WILL PLAGUE THEM UNTIL THEY DIE.
AND THOUGH HE NOW LIES ENTOMBED IN THE CRYPT BELOW THIS HALL, QUITE DEAD AND HARMLESS, HIS CURSE LIVES ON.

WHY WOULD LANCELOT CURSE HIS FELLOW KNIGHTS? ***HE*** WAS THE ONE WHO WRONGED ***THEM!***
NAY, LADY. LANCELOT NEVER BETRAYED ***ARTHUR***, NOR DID GUINEVERE.
THEY LOVED EACH OTHER, TRUE ENOUGH. BUT NEITHER ONE WOULD HAVE CUCKOLDED ARTHUR, FOR THEY LOVED HIM MORE THAN THEY LOVED EACH OTHER.

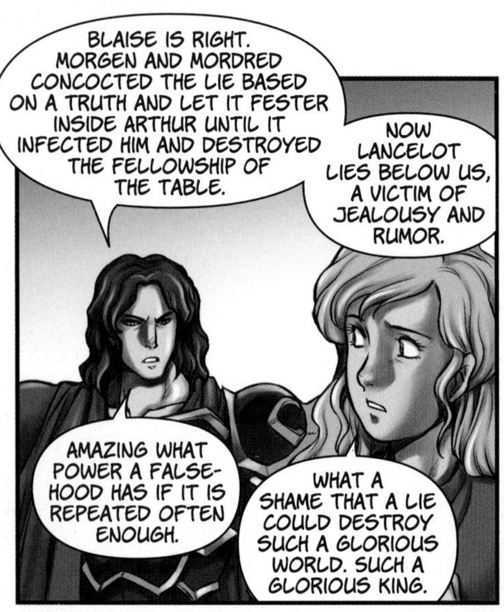
BLAISE IS RIGHT. MORGEN AND MORDRED CONCOCTED THE LIE BASED ON A TRUTH AND LET IT FESTER INSIDE ARTHUR UNTIL IT INFECTED HIM AND DESTROYED THE FELLOWSHIP OF THE TABLE.
NOW LANCELOT LIES BELOW US, A VICTIM OF JEALOUSY AND RUMOR.
AMAZING WHAT POWER A FALSE-HOOD HAS IF IT IS REPEATED OFTEN ENOUGH.
WHAT A SHAME THAT A LIE COULD DESTROY SUCH A GLORIOUS WORLD. SUCH A GLORIOUS KING.

WILL YOU TAKE ME TO SEE LANCELOT'S GRAVE?
IS IT POSSIBLE THAT MY LADY HAS A DEGREE OF MORBIDITY?
NAY. I WOULD JUST LIKE TO SEE THE RESTING PLACE OF A MAN SO REVERED AND SO SLANDERED.
AYE, LADY. I WILL TAKE YOU.
YES, WHY DON'T WE DO THAT, MY OH, SO EVIL KING.
SHUT UP, BLAISE. YOU'RE NOT INVITED.

WHOOSH
WHERE ARE WE? IT IS SO COLD!
IN LANCELOT'S CRYPT, FAR BELOW THE CASTLE'S FOUNDATION. SOME SAY THIS CHAPEL IS EMBEDDED IN A WALL OF ICE.

HERE LIES INTERRED THE RENOWNED LANCELOT DU LAC...
DID YOU KNOW HIM?

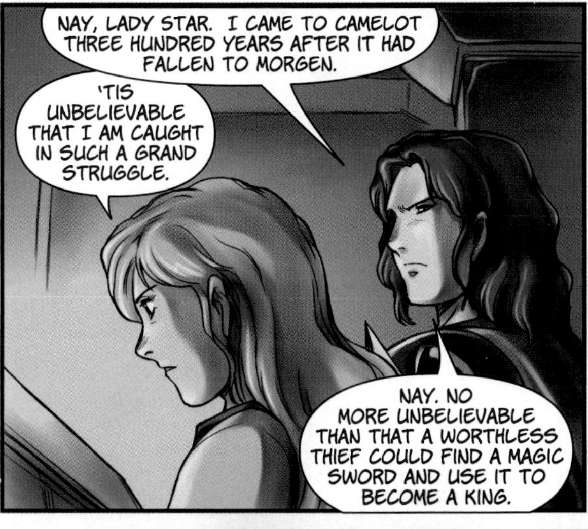
NAY, LADY STAR. I CAME TO CAMELOT THREE HUNDRED YEARS AFTER IT HAD FALLEN TO MORGEN.
'TIS UNBELIEVABLE THAT I AM CAUGHT IN SUCH A GRAND STRUGGLE.
NAY. NO MORE UNBELIEVABLE THAN THAT A WORTHLESS THIEF COULD FIND A MAGIC SWORD AND USE IT TO BECOME A KING.

IS THAT REALLY WHAT YOU WERE?
AYE. I WAS FLEEING THE GALLOWS WHEN I FOUND MY SWORD AND DREW IT FROM ITS RESTING PLACE IN THE FOREST.
ONE MOMENT I WAS RUNNING FROM SOLDIERS, THE NEXT I HAD MORE POWER THAN A MAN CAN DREAM OF.
WHAT IS TO BECOME OF YOU NOW THAT YOU HAVE BETRAYED MORGEN?
I KNOW NOT, MOUSE. IF I WERE A WISE MAN, I WOULD RETURN YOU TO HER.

BUT I'M NOT WISE.
TELL ME, SEREN, WHEN YOU DREAM ALL ALONE IN YOUR BED, WHAT MAN DO YOU SEE IN YOUR ARMS? IS IT A MAN LIKE LANCELOT?
NAY. NO ONE SO GRAND. I'VE NEVER SEEN HIS FACE, ONLY A VAGUE IMAGE OF HIM.
A QUIET MAN WITH A GOOD HEART.
ONE WHO IS RESPECTABLE AND CHARITABLE AND KIND.

AYE. I SUPPOSE A MOUSE LIKE YOU *WOULD* DREAM OF SUCH A MAN.
BUT...
COME. I'LL SHOW YOU TO YOUR CHAMBERS.
BUT I DIDN'T MEAN...
AYE, LADY. I THINK YOU DID.

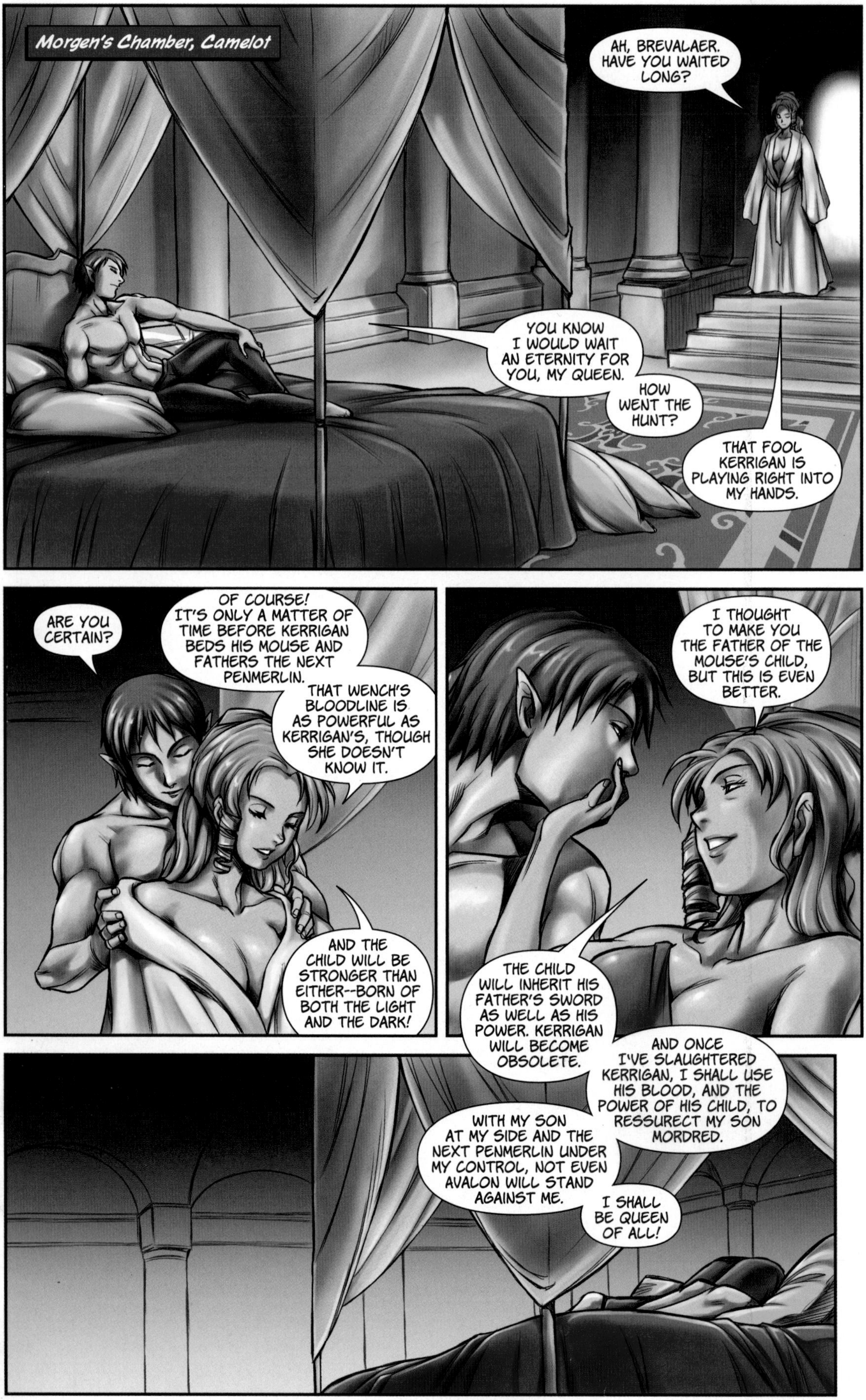

Morgen's Chamber, Camelot
AH, BREVALAER. HAVE YOU WAITED LONG?
YOU KNOW I WOULD WAIT AN ETERNITY FOR YOU, MY QUEEN.
HOW WENT THE HUNT?
THAT FOOL KERRIGAN IS PLAYING RIGHT INTO MY HANDS.

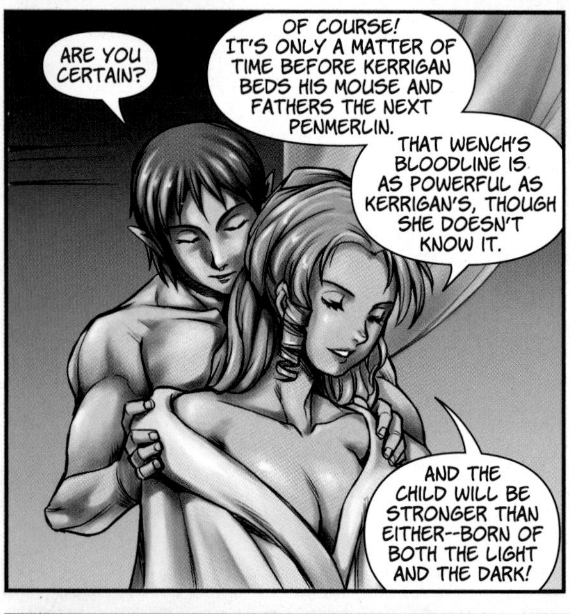

ARE YOU CERTAIN?
OF COURSE! IT'S ONLY A MATTER OF TIME BEFORE KERRIGAN BEDS HIS MOUSE AND FATHERS THE NEXT PENMERLIN.
THAT WENCH'S BLOODLINE IS AS POWERFUL AS KERRIGAN'S, THOUGH SHE DOESN'T KNOW IT.
AND THE CHILD WILL BE STRONGER THAN EITHER--BORN OF BOTH THE LIGHT AND THE DARK!

I THOUGHT TO MAKE YOU THE FATHER OF THE MOUSE'S CHILD, BUT THIS IS EVEN BETTER.
THE CHILD WILL INHERIT HIS FATHER'S SWORD AS WELL AS HIS POWER. KERRIGAN WILL BECOME OBSOLETE.

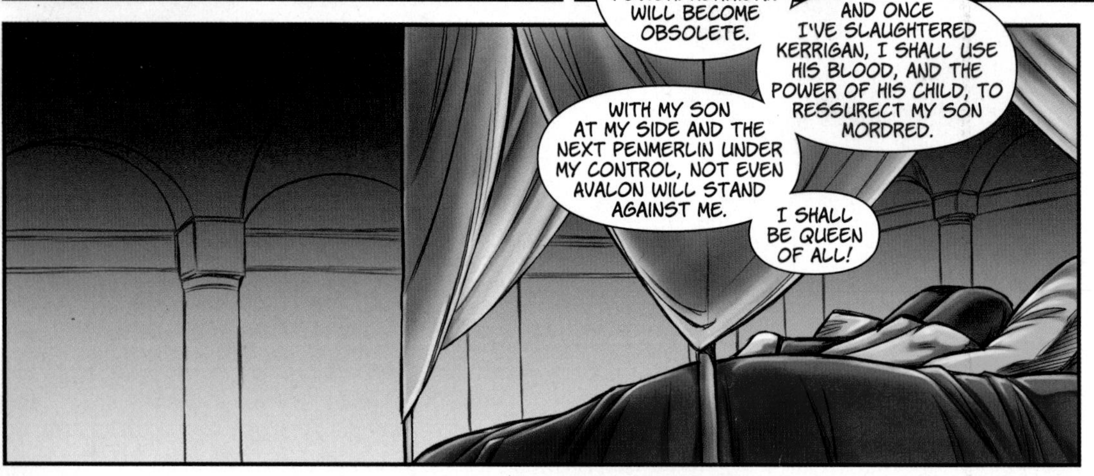

AND ONCE I'VE SLAUGHTERED KERRIGAN, I SHALL USE HIS BLOOD, AND THE POWER OF HIS CHILD, TO RESSURECT MY SON MORDRED.
WITH MY SON AT MY SIDE AND THE NEXT PENMERLIN UNDER MY CONTROL, NOT EVEN AVALON WILL STAND AGAINST ME.
I SHALL BE QUEEN OF ALL!

Lancelot's Chamber, Joyous Gard

THANK YOU, MY LORD.

FOR?

FOR SAVING ME FROM MORGEN, AND FOR GIVING ME SUCH A BEAUTIFUL ROOM.

THE CHAMBER WAS LANCELOT'S, NOT MINE. NOW YOU SHOULD REST.

WHAT OF YOU? WHERE WILL YOU SLEEP?

I DON'T. LONG AGO I LEARNED THAT SLEEPING MEN ARE EASY PREY, SO I NEVER SHUT MY EYES FOR MORE THAN A FEW MOMENTS AT A TIME.

I SUPPOSE THIS IS GOOD NIGHT, THEN.

SLEEP WELL. I HOPE YOU DREAM OF YOUR GENTLE MERCHANT'S KISSES.

OH!

WHAT'S WRONG? IS SOMETHING AMISS?

MY SCARLET CLOTH! I LEFT IT IN CAMELOT!

I CAN'T BELIEVE IT! IT'S LOST NOW. FOREVER!
IT'S ONLY CLOTH, MOUSE.
NO! IT WAS MINE. EVERY NIGHT FOR A FULL YEAR I WOVE IT ON MY MOTHER'S SMALL LOOM, WHEN EVERYONE ELSE IN THE HOUSE WAS ABED.

I SPENT EVERY COIN I HAD ON IT, EVERY SPARE MOMENT OF MY LIFE. IT MEANT EVERYTHING TO ME. EVERYTHING!
SLAM!
SILLY WENCH.

SILLY WENCH. WHY SHOULD I CARE ABOUT HER OR HER CLOTH?
I DON'T KNOW, LORD. WHY SHOULD YOU?
BLAISE, HOW MANY TIMES HAVE I TOLD YOU NOT TO SNEAK UP ON ME LIKE THAT?
MY HAND IS FASTER THAN MY MIND. ONE DAY I'LL KILL YOU WITHOUT MEANING TO.
SORRY.
WATCH THE WENCH FOR A BIT. THERE IS SOME-THING I NEED TO DO.
WHY DO I HAVE THIS SINKING FEELING THAT YOU'RE ABOUT TO DO SOMETHING VERY STUPID?
PROBABLY BECAUSE I AM.
THEN I SHALL GUARD HER ZEALOUSLY RATHER THAN JOIN YOU IN SAID STUPIDITY, AS I TRY MY BEST TO AVOID SUCH MOMENTS.
ACCERO, ACCERO DOMINA...

IT EVEN SMELLS OF HER...

WELL, WELL, MY HEARTLESS CHAMPION. WHO WOULD HAVE THOUGHT YOU WOULD BECOME SUCH A ROMANTIC?
AND SO OFTEN ROMANTICS DIE FOR THEIR LOVERS, DON'T THEY SWEET BREVALAER?
YES, MY QUEEN.
LET'S MAKE SURE THAT KERRIGAN ISN'T AN EXCEPTION TO THE RULE.

MOTHER, MOTHER, I WANT TO GO HOME!
WE WILL, SEREN DEAR. BUT FIRST WE MUST HELP THIS POOR CREATURE.
NO, MOTHER! HE WANTS TO EAT US!
NO, DARLING. HE IS IN PAIN AND HE IS AFRAID. IF WE APPROACH HIM CAREFULLY, HE WILL DO US NO HARM.
WE MEAN YOU NO HARM, WOLF. HERE. THIS WAS TO BE OUR LUNCH, BUT YOU NEED IT MORE THAN WE DO.

ONE DAY, MY SEREN, YOU'LL FIND ANOTHER WILD BEAST SUCH AS THIS ONE.
REMEMBER THAT NO MATTER HOW FERAL HE SEEMS AND NO MATTER HOW MUCH HE SNAPS, HE IS ONLY TRYING TO PROTECT HIMSELF.
IT WILL TAKE TIME TO SHOW HIM THAT YOU ONLY WANT TO HELP.
BUT ONCE HE LEARNS THAT YOU MEAN HIM NO HARM, HE WILL BE YOURS ALONE AND HE WILL FIGHT TO THE DEATH TO PROTECT YOU.
MOTHER!

LORD KERRIGAN? IS THAT YOU? DID YOU GO BACK TO CAMELOT TO FETCH MY CLOTH?
AYE, LADY. I TOLD YOU I WAS A THIEF.
PLEASE MY LORD, SHOW YOURSELF TO ME.
WHY?
I SHOULD LIKE TO THANK YOU FOR THIS, FACE TO FACE.
KEEP YOUR THANKS, WOMAN. IT'S AS WORTHLESS AS YOUR CLOTH.

NO! PLEASE DON'T GO!
BANG!

I MUST THANK HIM.
BUT HOW?

I'LL MAKE HIM A TUNIC.

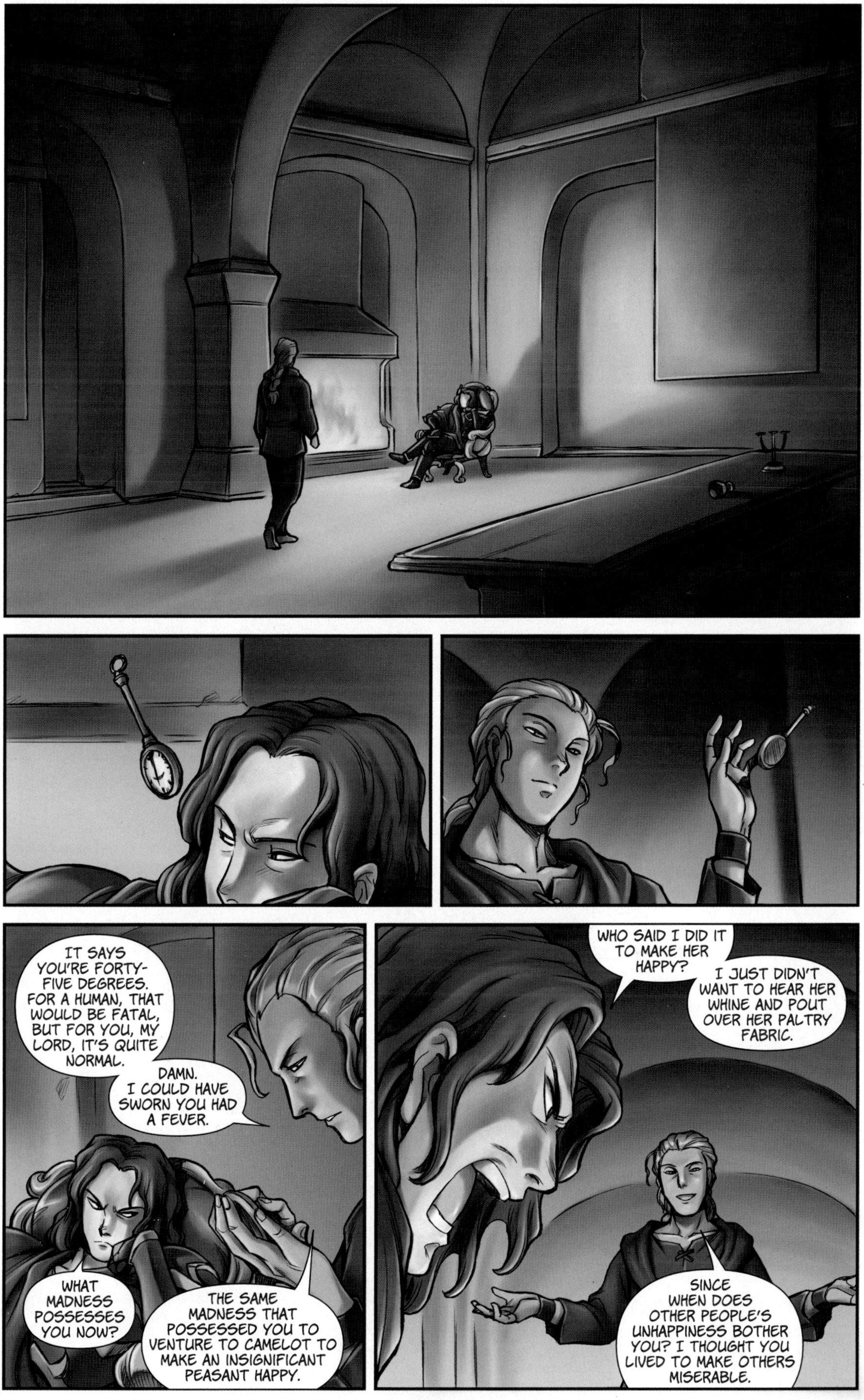

IT SAYS YOU'RE FORTY-FIVE DEGREES. FOR A HUMAN, THAT WOULD BE FATAL, BUT FOR YOU, MY LORD, IT'S QUITE NORMAL.
DAMN. I COULD HAVE SWORN YOU HAD A FEVER.
WHAT MADNESS POSSESSES YOU NOW?
THE SAME MADNESS THAT POSSESSED YOU TO VENTURE TO CAMELOT TO MAKE AN INSIGNIFICANT PEASANT HAPPY.

WHO SAID I DID IT TO MAKE HER HAPPY?
I JUST DIDN'T WANT TO HEAR HER WHINE AND POUT OVER HER PALTRY FABRIC.
SINCE WHEN DOES OTHER PEOPLE'S UNHAPPINESS BOTHER YOU? I THOUGHT YOU LIVED TO MAKE OTHERS MISERABLE.

IT FEELS GOOD, DOESN'T IT?

WHAT?

TO DO SOMETHING DECENT FOR ANOTHER. YOU'VE NEVER DONE THAT BEFORE, HAVE YOU?

YOU OVERSTEP YOUR BOUNDS, SERVANT!

DO SO AGAIN AND PERISH.

AS YOU WISH, MY MOST CRUEL AND EVIL KING.

LA, LA,
LA, LA, LA...

SEREN? I'VE BROUGHT YOU SOME SUPPER.

THANK YOU, BLAISE. COULD YOU SET IT ASIDE PLEASE? I'M NOT HUNGRY YET.

YOU WORK WITHOUT A PATTERN AND WITHOUT MEASUREMENTS?
AYE. WHEN I'M IN MY WORKING TRANCE I DON'T NEED THEM. MASTER RUFUS CALLED IT MY MAGIC.
I'M SURE HE DID.

SEREN?
AYE?
WHO WERE YOUR PARENTS?
MY MOTHER WAS A WEAVER; I WOVE THIS CLOTH ON HER LOOM. I KNOW NOTHING OF MY FATHER. HE DIED SHORTLY BEFORE I WAS BORN.
AND YOUR MOTHER? WHERE IS SHE NOW?

SHE DIED NOT LONG AFTER I WAS APPRENTICED TO MASTER RUFUS. IT WAS AN ACCIDENT. A FIRE BROKE OUT IN HER ROOM WHILE SHE WAS SLEEPING.
ARE YOU CERTAIN HER DEATH WAS AN ACCIDENT?

FORGIVE ME, MY LADY. IT WAS A THOUGHTLESS QUESTION.
YOU SHOULD EAT YOUR FOOD BEFORE IT GROWS COLD.

SOMEHOW, SEREN, I DON'T THINK YOUR MOTHER'S DEATH WAS AN ACCIDENT.

IT WILL MATCH HIS EYES WHEN THEY BURN RED!

SEREN?!

(4)

Joyous Gard
SEREN... OH, SEREN!
LITTLE MOUSE! WHAT DID YOU THINK YOU WERE DOING?!
GIFT... FOR YOU...
BLAISE! I NEED YOU!

GODS!
DID MORGEN
DO THIS?
NAY. SEREN
SURPRISED ME AS
I DOZED.

MY MAGIC
CANNOT HEAL;
IT CAN ONLY
HARM.

SAVE
HER!

ARRA TERAC
SISIMEA DOMINAY
NARAH...

YOU'RE LOSING HER!
ARRA TERAC SISIMEA DOMINAY NARAH! ARRA TERAC SISIMEA DOMINAY NARAH!

UHN...

SHE'S LOST A LOT OF BLOOD. SHE NEEDS REST.
AYE.

ACCERO, ACCERO DOMINA...

A DRESS TO MATCH YOUR INNOCENCE.

HA, HA, HA!
MOTHER?
YOU'VE CHANGED MUCH, MY LITTLE TREASURE.
I'VE MISSED YOU, MAMA.
I HAVE MISSED YOU TOO, MY SEREN.
I'VE HEARD YOU WHISPERING TO ME MANY TIMES AND HAVE WANTED TO ANSWER YOU BUT COULDN'T. NOT UNTIL NOW.
AM I DEAD?
NO. MERELY SLEEPING.
THEN WHY ARE YOU HERE, MAMA?
THIS HAS BEEN IN OUR FAMILY FOR GENERATIONS, MY SEREN.
LIKE THE LOOM I GAVE TO YOU, IT BELONGED TO MY MOTHER AND TO HERS BEFORE HER. NOW I'M GIFTING IT TO YOU. IT'S PAST TIME FOR YOU TO HAVE IT.
IT LOOKS LIKE THE MEDALLION KERRIGAN WEARS.
AYE, SEREN. ALL THOSE DESCENDED FROM THE ORIGINAL THIRTEEN WAREMERLINS BEAR THEM.
YOUR ANCESTOR WAS EMRYS PENMERLIN, THE ONE WHO BETRAYED HIS KING AND SET ALL THIS EVIL IN MOTION. NOW OUR BLOODLINE MUST SAVE THE WORLD FROM MORGEN AND HER DEMONS.
I DON'T UNDERSTAND.
YOU WILL WHEN THE TIME COMES.
DON'T CRY, SEREN. NOT FOR ME. I'M AT PEACE. WHEN YOU WAKE, YOU MAY NOT REMEMBER THIS DREAM. BUT YOU WILL FIND THE MEDALLION WHEN YOU NEED IT.

A GIFT... FOR ME.
I WANT NO GIFTS.
I WILL NOT LEAVE MY HEART OPEN TO BE RAVAGED BY ANOTHER.
I AM NO WOMAN'S PAWN!

I'LL BURN IT!

BUT SUCH CRAFTSMANSHIP!
MY LITTLE MOUSE IS TALENTED.

AND IT SMELLS OF HER!

A GIFT... FOR ME.
THANK YOU, SEREN.
YOU WILL NEVER KNOW I WEAR IT, BUT I THANK YOU JUST THE SAME.

WHEN WILL YOU WAKE, SEREN?
I NEED TO KNOW YOU ARE WELL, BUT I DON'T WANT YOU TO SEE ME. NOT YET.
NOT AFTER...

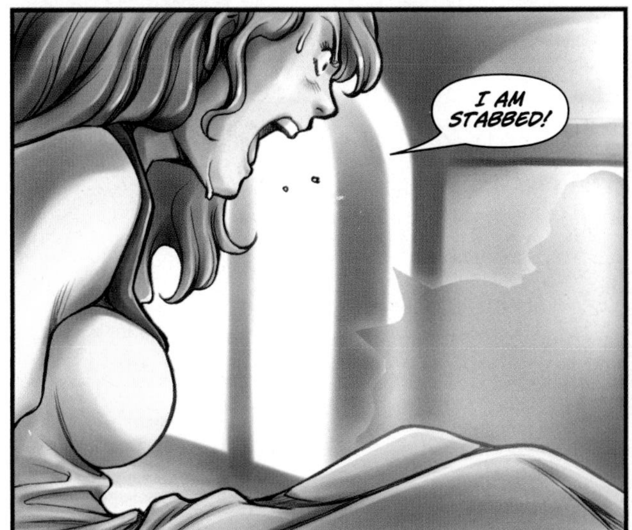
I AM STABBED!

BUT WHERE'S THE BLOOD?

BUT WHERE IS THE WOUND?
DID I DREAM IT?
NAY! KERRIGAN STABBED ME! I'M SURE OF IT!

BUT I FEEL NO PAIN...
DID HE HEAL ME?

KERRIGAN, IS THAT YOU? IF YOU'RE HERE, LET ME SEE YOU!

OH... KERRIGAN!

DID I HURT YOU?
NAY! UNLESS YOU'VE TURNED ME WANTON!
YOU ARE STILL A MAIDEN, SEREN. I DID NOT TAKE YOUR VIRGINITY FROM YOU.

NAY, MY LORD. YOU DID NOT TAKE MY VIRGINITY BUT I WISH TO GIVE IT TO YOU.

DO YOU KNOW WHAT YOU OFFER, LADY STAR?
NO LORD OF AVALON WILL HAVE YOU ONCE YOU'VE BEEN DEFILED BY ME.
I DON'T WANT TO BE THE BRIDE OF SOME NAMELESS KNIGHT.
I WANT TO MAKE MY OWN CHOICES.
AND I CHOOSE YOU.
IS THIS THE GIFT YOU WOULD GIVE ME, LADY STAR?
AYE, MY LORD.
YOU ACCEPT A DEMON AS YOUR LOVER?
ONLY IF THE DEMON IS YOU.
OPEN YOUR EYES, LADY STAR.
I WANT YOU TO SEE ME TAKE YOUR GIFT SO THAT YOU CAN NEVER ACCUSE ME OF HAVING STOLEN IT FROM YOU.
NAY, KERRIGAN. I'VE OFFERED MYSELF TO YOU.
WHY SHOULD I FAULT YOU FOR MY ACTIONS?
AND PERHAPS, AFTER ALL, THIS IS MY DESTINY...

ONE OF MORGEN'S SCOUTS!

TIME TO CHANGE...

...AND TO FIGHT, DRAGON AGAINST DRAGON!

HA! IS THAT THE BEST YOU CAN DO?
YOU PATHETIC LITTLE...
WINGED WORM!
MY WING!
TAKE THAT!
AAAHHHH!
WE'RE IN FOR IT NOW!
LORD KERRIGAN, COME QUICKLY! WE'RE UNDER ATTACK!

HOW DID THEY FIND US?
DON'T LOOK AT ME. I WAS CLEANING UP SEREN'S BLOOD WHEN I FELT THE PULL OF MY KIND APPROACHING.
WHAT WERE *YOU* DOING?
NOTHING THAT SHOULD HAVE CAUSED THIS.
SOMEHOW I DOUBT THAT.
SHUT UP, BLAISE. I NEED TO RAISE A SHIELD...
ACCERO, ACCERO DOMINI DOYAN...
OOOFF!
THUNK!
THAT SHOULD TAKE CARE OF THINGS.
YES, AS LONG AS YOU REMAIN STRONG.
BUT AS SOON AS YOU FALL ASLEEP OR GROW WEAK FROM HUNGER, THEY'LL BE UPON US.
AND WE BOTH KNOW WHAT YOU FEED ON, KERRIGAN.
WHAT WILL YOU DO—DRAIN SEREN?

THE CASTLE IS UNDER ATTACK BUT I CAN DO NOTHING!
KERRIGAN?? YOU'VE COME BACK FOR ME!

SEREN? ARE YOU ALL RIGHT?
H-HOW DO YOU KNOW MY NAME?
I KNOW THE NAME OF EVERY-ONE WHO COMES TO MY HOME.
YOUR HOME?
YOU'RE LANCELOT?

AYE, MY LADY, AND I'M HERE TO PROTECT YOU.
I AM GLAD TO HEAR IT, MY LORD.
NO DOUBT LORD KERRIGAN COULD USE ANOTHER SWORD, EVEN IF IT DOES BELONG TO A GHOST.

KERRIGAN?
HE IS THE BEAST THAT I'M HERE TO PROTECT YOU FROM!

KERRIGAN IS NO BEAST! HE IS TRYING TO KEEP ME SAFE.
NAY, MY LADY. I DON'T THINK YOU QUITE COMPREHEND THE POSITION YOU'RE IN.
AYE, BUT I DO. MORGEN WANTS TO CAPTURE ME SO THAT SHE CAN USE ME TO GET THE ROUND TABLE AND DESTROY THE WORLD. KERRIGAN IS SAVING ME FROM MORGEN.

POOR LADY SEREN. YOU DON'T UNDERSTAND WHAT YOU HAVE DONE THIS DAY, DO YOU?
AND WHAT HAVE I DONE?
YOU TOOK THE DEVIL INTO YOUR BED AND NOW YOU CARRY HIS CHILD.

NAY. 'TIS NOT POSSIBLE!
AYE, BUT IT IS. I CAN FEEL THE LIFE FORCE OF THE BABY THAT IS BEGINNING TO FORM EVEN NOW. AND ONCE KERRIGAN LEARNS THAT YOU CARRY HIS CHILD, HE WILL DESTROY IT.
NAY!
AYE, LADY. LONG AGO, LORD KERRIGAN WAS CURSED BY MORGEN. HE DOESN'T EAT AS WE DO. HE LIVES OFF THE BLOOD OF CHILDREN. THAT ALONE SUSTAINS HIM.

I DON'T BELIEVE YOU!
I'M ON YOUR SIDE IN THIS MATTER, SEREN.
KERRIGAN IS A POWERFUL DEMON WHO CAN COMMAND THE ELEMENTS. HE'S EVIL TO THE MARROW OF HIS BONES.
YOU WILL ONLY SURVIVE IF YOU TRUST ME.
KILL KERRIGAN, AND THEN STEAL HIS SWORD AND SCABBARD AND GIVE THEM TO ME. THEN I'LL TAKE YOU TO A PLACE WHERE YOU AND YOUR BABE WILL BE SAFE.

I DON'T TRUST YOU.
YOU SAY YOU'LL HELP ME IF I KILL KERRIGAN AND STEAL HIS SWORD FOR YOU.
EVEN IF I DIDN'T KILL HIM, STEALING HIS SWORD WOULD LEAVE HIM DEFENSELESS.
ANYONE WHO WAS TRULY GOOD WOULD OFFER TO HELP ME WITHOUT CONDITION.
ANYONE WHO WAS TRULY GOOD WOULDN'T ASK ME TO KILL.

YOU FEEBLEMINDED WOMAN! GO AHEAD AND THROW YOUR LOT IN WITH YOUR DEVIL--

--AND WHEN HE DEVOURS YOU AND YOUR CHILD, REMEMBER THAT YOU WERE OFFERED THE CHANCE TO SAVE BOTH YOUR LIVES!

WHO ARE YOU?

WHO AM I, YOU IMBECILIC CHIT? I AM BREA OF THE TUATHA DE DANAAN AND I HAVE COME TO RECLAIM THE SWORD CALIBURN.

IT WAS A SWORD FORGED BY THE GODS AND TO THE GODS IT MUST BE RETURNED. WE ARE TIRED OF SEEING IT MISUSED!

SHRACK

KERRACK

AHHH! I WON'T BE ABLE TO HOLD THE SHIELD FOR MUCH LONGER! NOT UNDER SUCH CONDITIONS!
BUT IF I LET IT DROP WE ARE DOOMED!

I MUST REST, BUT I MUST CONSERVE MY MAGIC.
DO I EVEN REMEMBER HOW TO UNDRESS LIKE A MORTAL MAN?

CLANG!
CLANNG!

HAVING PROBLEMS?
NO. WHY?
YOU'RE MAKING A RACKET.
SO?

OOOH... RED! WHAT A DIFFERENT LOOK FOR YOU, OH DARK ONE WHO ALWAYS WEARS BLACK.
PUT IT DOWN, BLAISE.

NO WAY. IF YOU'RE SO LOW ON POWER THAT YOU'RE NOT USING MAGIC TO UNDRESS, THEN I KNOW YOU WON'T TAKE A SHOT AT ME OR CHOKE ME.
I MAY NEVER GET THE CHANCE TO TAUNT YOU AGAIN WITHOUT RISKING BODILY INJURY.
BLAISE, I REALLY HATE YOU.
I KNOW.

NOW WATCH ME CLOSELY. HERE'S HOW YOU DRESS. YOU PUT YOUR ARMS IN LIKE THIS, PULL IT OVER YOUR HEAD, AND THEN YOU SETTLE IT ON YOUR BODY.
"SEE?"
YOU KNOW WHY ARMIES WEAR THAT COLOR RED, DON'T YOU?

NO. WHY?
IT HIDES BLOODSTAINS.

WHAT THE HELL?
HOW CAN THIS BE? I SAW SEREN SEW THIS FABRIC! THERE'S NO METAL IN IT!

I KNEW IT!
KNEW WHAT?
SEREN WOVE MAGIC INTO THIS GARMENT. YOUR LITTLE MOUSE IS A MERLIN!

SO HOW ARE YOU GOING TO BREAK THE NEWS TO HER?

GOOD QUESTION, BLAISE. WHAT CAN I SAY TO HER?
KERRIGAN?

WHAT IS THAT?
DANDELION SALAD WITH COWSLIP AND BERRIES. IT WAS ALL I COULD FIND IN THE KITCHEN GARDENS. I THOUGHT YOU MIGHT BE HUNGRY.
NAY, SEREN.
YOU HAVEN'T EATEN ANYTHING ALL DAY.
I'M QUITE FINE WITHOUT.

YOU CAN'T GO WITHOUT FOOD.
I CAN'T EAT THOSE.
THEN WHAT WOULD YOU LIKE? YOU MUST EAT SOMETHING.
WHAT IS THIS REALLY ABOUT?
I KNOW NOT WHAT YOU MEAN.
YOU DO. TELL ME.

I... I HEARD THAT YOU FEED FROM THE BLOOD OF CHILDREN.
NAY, LITTLE MOUSE. I FIND NOTHING NOURISHING ABOUT THE BLOOD OF CHILDREN.

THEN WHAT WOULD YOU LIKE TO EAT?

WHAT I LIKE TO EAT, LITTLE MOUSE, IS LIFE.

I DON'T UNDERSTAND.
THINK, SEREN. HAVEN'T YOU WONDERED WHY I'M SO COLD TO THE TOUCH?
AYE, BUT...
DON'T YOU WANT TO KNOW WHAT WARMS ME?
...NAY.
IN ORDER TO LIVE I DRAIN LIFE.
I DON'T UNDERSTAND...
I FEED ON THE ELECTRICITY OF THE HUMAN HEART—I SUCK IT INTO MY BODY...
LIKE THIS...
IT HURTS!
AYE, LITTLE MOUSE.
BUT IF ONLY YOU COULD FEEL THE RUSH OF WHAT I FEEL!
AND I ONLY TAKE A MOUTHFUL OF YOUR LIFE!
WHAT HAPPENS TO THOSE YOU DRAW FROM?
IF THEY'RE HUMAN, THEY DIE. IF THEY ARE ADONI, THEY CAN SURVIVE IT, AT LEAST ON OCCASION.
YOU KILL PEOPLE AND STEAL THEIR SOULS?
NAY, LITTLE MOUSE! THE SOUL HOLDS NOTHING FOR ME. GIVE IT TO YOUR GOD OR YOUR DEVIL. I CARE NOT WHICH.
AND AS FOR DEATH... BETTER THEM THAN ME!
THE SHIELD! IT'S BREACHED!

MORGEN'S GARGOYLES!
GRARRR!
RUN, SEREN!
RUN!

Joyous Gard

RUN, SEREN!

KERBANG!
KAFF KAFF
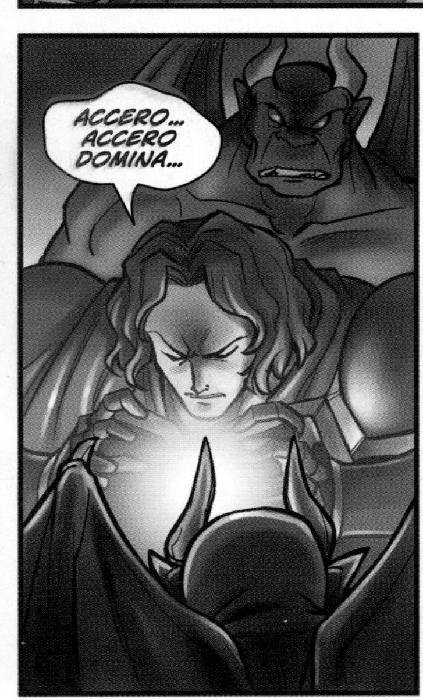
ACCERO... ACCERO DOMINA...

WHAT THE...?
HEY, WAIT A MINUTE...

YOU'RE SAFE, SEREN. THEY'RE GONE NOW.
HOW DID THEY GET INSIDE THE SHIELD?

WHEN I TOOK THE SPARK OF LIFE FROM YOU, IT OPENED A SLIT IN THE SHIELD.
I CAN'T FEED AND HOLD THE SHIELD AT THE SAME TIME. NOT UNLESS I WISH TO KILL YOU.
CAN'T YOU JUST FLASH US OUT OF HERE THE WAY YOU FLASHED US IN?

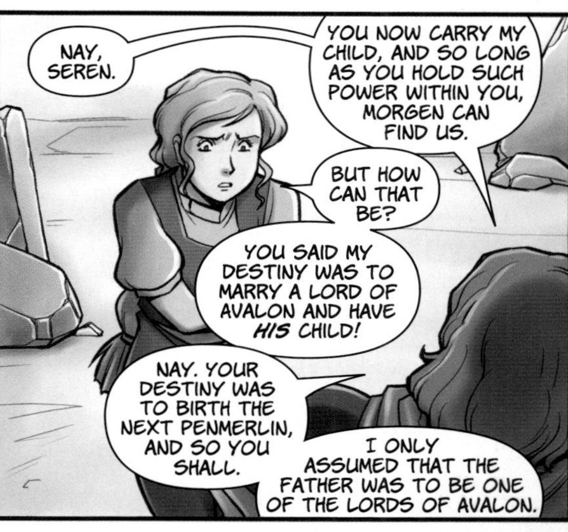
NAY, SEREN.
YOU NOW CARRY MY CHILD, AND SO LONG AS YOU HOLD SUCH POWER WITHIN YOU, MORGEN CAN FIND US.
BUT HOW CAN THAT BE?
YOU SAID MY DESTINY WAS TO MARRY A LORD OF AVALON AND HAVE *HIS* CHILD!
NAY. YOUR DESTINY WAS TO BIRTH THE NEXT PENMERLIN, AND SO YOU SHALL.
I ONLY ASSUMED THAT THE FATHER WAS TO BE ONE OF THE LORDS OF AVALON.

IF MORGEN TAKES YOU NOW, SHE WILL HAVE POSSESSION OF ONE OF THE MOST POWERFUL BEINGS ON EARTH.
WITH YOUR CHILD IN HER THRALL, SHE WILL BE ABLE TO RESURRECT MORDRED AND DEFEAT AVALON.
THROUGH THE BABE SHE WILL BE ABLE TO CONTROL MY SWORD, CALIBURN. HENCE EVEN I WILL BE... UNNECESSARY.
I HAVE SIRED MY HEIR... AND MY DOOM.

BUT IT IS OUR CHILD.
AYE. AND BY USING HIS POWER MYSELF I WILL BE ABLE TO RULE THE WORLDS OF MAN AND MAGE AND BRING THEM BOTH TO THEIR KNEES!
YOU WOULD USE YOUR CHILD TO FURTHER YOUR OWN ENDS?

THERE IS NO LOYALTY IN BLOOD. WHEN I WAS TEN YEARS OLD MY OWN MOTHER TRIED TO SELL ME TO THE HIGHEST BIDDER AND I MURDERED HER FOR IT.
I WILL DO WHATEVER I MUST TO REMAIN WHERE I AM.
I WON'T GO BACK TO BEING A POWERLESS PAUPER!
NAY! YOU MIGHT NOT BELIEVE IN THE LOYALTY OF BLOOD, BUT I DO!
I WILL FIGHT TO PROTECT THIS CHILD, EVEN IF IT MEANS FIGHTING YOU!

YOU—BATTLE ME?
I COULD BREAK YOU IN TWAIN WITH MY BARE HANDS!
THEN YOU WILL HAVE TO DO IT, MY LORD.
FOR I WILL NOT STAND QUIETLY BY WHILE YOU BARTER THE LIFE OF MY CHILD FOR YOUR OWN POWER!

ALL PEOPLE ARE BORN WITH GOODNESS INSIDE THEM. ***ALL.*** AND I KNOW THAT SOMEWHERE DEEP INSIDE YOU THAT GOODNESS STILL EXISTS.
YOU WERE TENDER WITH ME WHEN YOU CREATED THIS CHILD.
I KNOW YOU CAN FIND THE SAME TENDERNESS FOR HIM.
DON'T LET HIM LEARN BRUTALITY FROM YOUR HANDS.

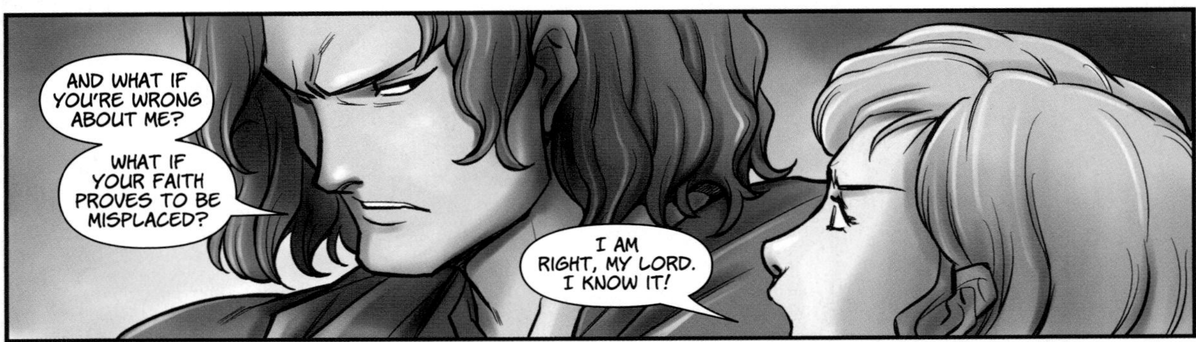

AND WHAT IF YOU'RE WRONG ABOUT ME?
WHAT IF YOUR FAITH PROVES TO BE MISPLACED?
I AM RIGHT, MY LORD. I KNOW IT!

THOOM

WHAT IS THAT?

IN SHORT, OUR DOOM.

NO!
SCREW THIS PAIN!
TAKE THAT!

HA!

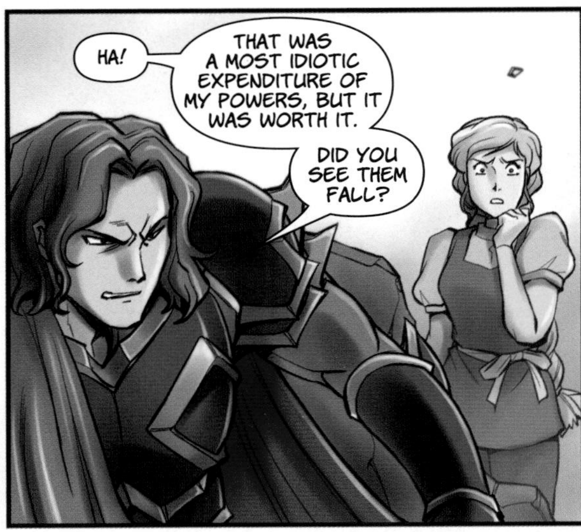
HA!
THAT WAS A MOST IDIOTIC EXPENDITURE OF MY POWERS, BUT IT WAS WORTH IT.
DID YOU SEE THEM FALL?

AYE, MY LORD.
IT WAS QUITE LOVELY THE WAY THEY HURTLED THROUGH THE AIR.
BUT DID IT GAIN YOU ANYTHING?
NOTHING BUT SATISFACTION, AND THERE IS MUCH TO BE SAID FOR THAT.

ARE YOU ALL RIGHT?
I'M NOT FALLEN OR DEFEATED YET.
BUT REMIND ME NOT TO DO THAT AGAIN.
DOES IT HURT?
ONLY WHEN I MOVE...OR BREATHE.
NOW IF YOU'LL EXCUSE ME, I SHOULD LIKE TO GO LIE DOWN FOR A BIT.

YOU'LL ADMIT THAT TO ME?
'TIS LESS DAMAGING TO MY EGO THAN PASSING OUT AND LESS DANGEROUS AS WELL.
THEN I SHALL LEAD YOU BACK TO YOUR ROOM.
UNLESS YOU WISH TO POP US THERE.
NAY. WE'LL HAVE TO USE OUR FEET.
I CAN'T AFFORD ANOTHER BLAST TO MY POWERS RIGHT NOW.

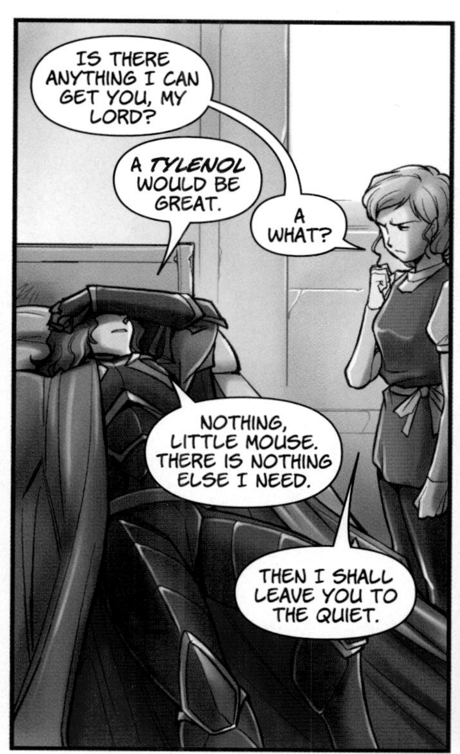
IS THERE ANYTHING I CAN GET YOU, MY LORD?
A *TYLENOL* WOULD BE GREAT.
A WHAT?
NOTHING, LITTLE MOUSE. THERE IS NOTHING ELSE I NEED.
THEN I SHALL LEAVE YOU TO THE QUIET.

NAY, SEREN. STAY WITH ME A WHILE.

I'M GROWING WEAKER, SEREN. I WON'T BE ABLE TO HOLD THE SHIELD PAST TOMORROW.
WHAT WILL MORGEN DO TO YOU ONCE SHE CAPTURES YOU?
I'M MORE CONCERNED ABOUT WHAT SHE WILL DO TO YOU.
MORGEN WON'T NEED YOU ONCE THE CHILD IS BORN.
MOST LIKELY SHE'LL CUT IT FROM YOU THE INSTANT IT'S ABLE TO LIVE ON ITS OWN.

THEN PROMISE ME TWO THINGS. PLEASE.
AYE?
PROMISE THAT YOU WILL PROTECT THE BABY FOR ME WHEN I AM GONE.
I MAY NOT BE HERE EITHER, SEREN.
BUT IF YOU ARE, PROMISE ME!
AYE. AND WHAT IS YOUR OTHER REQUEST?
MARRY ME IN SECRET.

MARRY YOU?
AYE. I WON'T BE HERE LONG ENOUGH FOR YOU TO WORRY OVER AND I DON'T EXPECT YOU TO HONOR THE VOWS, BUT I WANT MY CHILD BORN IN WEDLOCK.
SEREN—
PLEASE, KERRIGAN. FOR THE CHILD'S SAKE.

I WON'T DO IT FOR THIS CHILD, SEREN.
BUT I WILL DO IT FOR YOU.

Later...
KNOCK!

LORD KERRIGAN, I NEED A WORD WITH YOU.
WHAT??
GIVE US A MOMENT, BLAISE!
THAT MANDRAKE HAS ALWAYS HAD TERRIBLE TIMING!

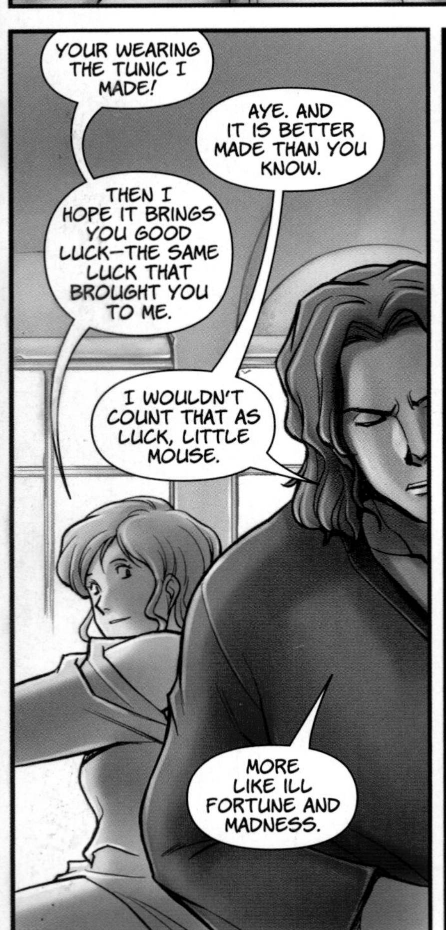
YOUR WEARING THE TUNIC I MADE!
AYE. AND IT IS BETTER MADE THAN YOU KNOW.
THEN I HOPE IT BRINGS YOU GOOD LUCK—THE SAME LUCK THAT BROUGHT YOU TO ME.
I WOULDN'T COUNT THAT AS LUCK, LITTLE MOUSE.
MORE LIKE ILL FORTUNE AND MADNESS.

WE HAVE A GARGOYLE AT THE GATE.
A GARGOYLE? YOU DISTURBED ME FOR THIS?
GOD'S BLOOD, HAVE YOU BEEN BY THE WINDOW LATELY? THERE'S AN ENTIRE ARMY FLYING OVER OUR HEADS!
I SAID A GARGOYLE IS AT THE GATE, NOT EIGHT HUNDRED.

WHAT DO YOU MEAN?
GARAFYN IS OUTSIDE, WANTING A PARLEY.
GARAFYN, KING OF THE GARGOYLES? DOES HE EVEN HAVE A TONGUE?
APPARENTLY SO.
HE'S A CRUSTY OLD BASTARD AND WANTS TO CHAT WITH YOU.
WHY?
HOW SHOULD I KNOW? I'M JUST THE SERVANT AND HE WON'T TALK TO ME.

WELL?
I AM HERE AT THE BEHEST OF THE QUEEN OF CAMELOT. I—
WHAT?
YOU KNOW, THE BITCH ON THE THRONE?
THE ONE WHO THINKS SHE'S THE GREATER EVIL, WHICH IS TRUE SINCE NO ONE ELSE IS A BIGGER BITCH, BUT THAT'S BESIDE THE POINT.

SHE WANTED ME TO TALK TO YOU SO HERE I AM, ROASTING IN THE SUN, AND PRAYING THAT ONE OF THOSE DAMNED DRAGONS DOESN'T LOB A GLOB OF $#@% ON MY SHOULDER. GOD KNOWS I GET ENOUGH OF THAT FROM THE PIGEONS.

THERE'S NOTHING EITHER OF YOU COULD POSSIBLY SAY THAT I WOULD CARE TO HEAR.
FINE. BUT TOMORROW WHEN THEY STRIP THAT SWORD FROM YOU AND DRAG YOUR CARCASS OFF IN CHAINS--
--CLUB THE WOMAN IN THE HEAD AND SLICE HER OPEN IN A FEW MONTHS' TIME, REMEMBER THAT THE GARGOYLE SCHMUCK TRIED TO TALK TO YOU, BUT YOU HAD BETTER THINGS TO DO LIKE GO PLAN A FUNERAL.

G'HEAD. HAVE A NICE DEATH.
GARAFYN?
YOU READY TO PARLEY?
DEPENDS ON WHAT YOU HAVE TO SAY.
OKAY, THEN. BUT YOU'D BETTER LOOK PISSED WHILE YOU LISTEN.

I'M TALKING TREASON AND THE BITCH AIN'T STUPID.
ACTING ISN'T YOUR FORTE.

I WON'T PLAY YOUR GAMES, GARAFYN. WHAT'S YOUR POINT?
THAT'S MUCH BETTER. THE OLD SNARLING KERRIGAN!

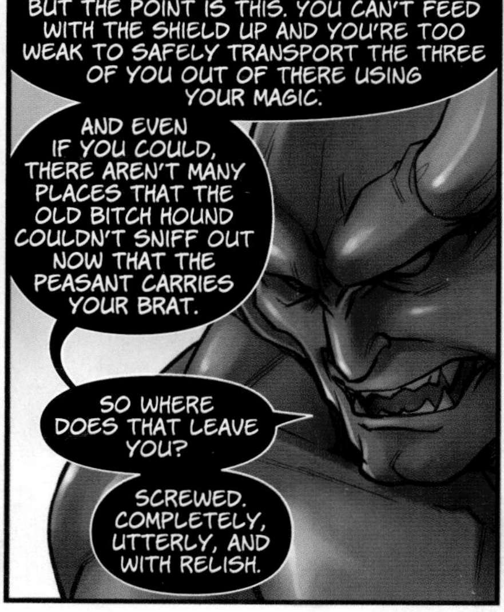
BUT THE POINT IS THIS. YOU CAN'T FEED WITH THE SHIELD UP AND YOU'RE TOO WEAK TO SAFELY TRANSPORT THE THREE OF YOU OUT OF THERE USING YOUR MAGIC.
AND EVEN IF YOU COULD, THERE AREN'T MANY PLACES THAT THE OLD BITCH HOUND COULDN'T SNIFF OUT NOW THAT THE PEASANT CARRIES YOUR BRAT.
SO WHERE DOES THAT LEAVE YOU?
SCREWED. COMPLETELY, UTTERLY, AND WITH RELISH.

BUT YOU KNOW SOMETHING? SCREWING MEN HAS NEVER BEEN TO MY TASTE. SO I'M THINKING ABOUT SOMETHING THAT WE'LL BOTH LIKE A WHOLE LOT BETTER.
AND THAT IS?
WE JOIN FORCES AND BETRAY THE BITCH.
HOW DO I KNOW I CAN TRUST YOU?
BASICALLY, YOU DON'T.
BUT WITHIN TWENTY-FOUR HOURS YOU'RE GONNA FALL AND EVERYBODY DOWN THERE KNOWS IT.

HENCE, TOMORROW I CAN LEAD MY STONE LEGION UP HERE AND RISK YOU CHISELING OFF A VITAL PIECE OF MY ANATOMY BEFORE YOU GO DOWN--
--OR ME AND A COUPLE OF MY FRIENDS CAN HOLD THE HORDE BACK LONG ENOUGH FOR YOU TO RECHARGE YOUR BATTERIES AND GET US ALL THE HELL OUT OF HERE.
AND IN RETURN YOU WANT MY MAGICAL MEDALLION?

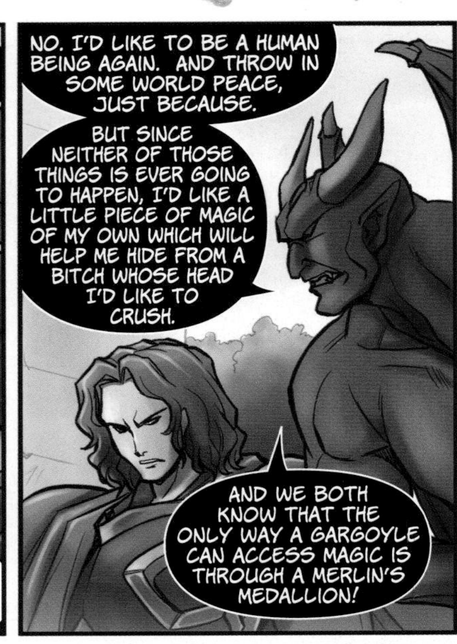
NO. I'D LIKE TO BE A HUMAN BEING AGAIN. AND THROW IN SOME WORLD PEACE, JUST BECAUSE.
BUT SINCE NEITHER OF THOSE THINGS IS EVER GOING TO HAPPEN, I'D LIKE A LITTLE PIECE OF MAGIC OF MY OWN WHICH WILL HELP ME HIDE FROM A BITCH WHOSE HEAD I'D LIKE TO CRUSH.
AND WE BOTH KNOW THAT THE ONLY WAY A GARGOYLE CAN ACCESS MAGIC IS THROUGH A MERLIN'S MEDALLION!

LOOK, I HAVE NO REAL BEEF WITH YOU EXCEPT FOR THE FACT THAT YOU'VE BEEN KNOWN TO BLOW A FEW OF US INTO DUST FOR NO PARTICULAR REASON.
BUT THEN AGAIN, I'VE BEEN KNOWN TO DO THE SAME WHEN MY FELLOW GARGOYLES PISS ME OFF.
SO I CAN LIVE WITH YOU AND YOUR TEMPER TANTRUMS.

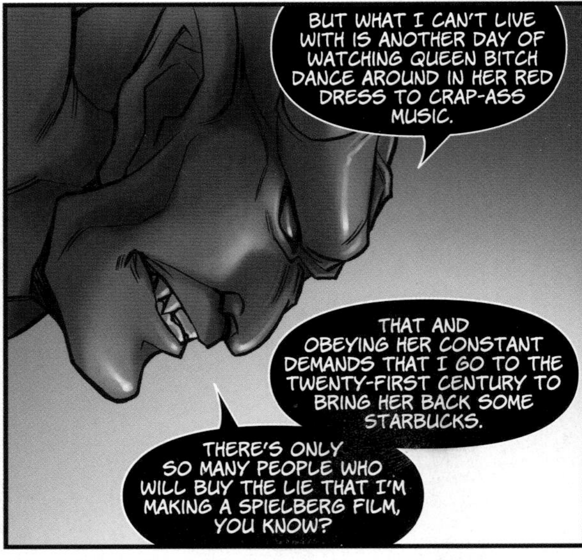
BUT WHAT I CAN'T LIVE WITH IS ANOTHER DAY OF WATCHING QUEEN BITCH DANCE AROUND IN HER RED DRESS TO CRAP-ASS MUSIC.
THAT AND OBEYING HER CONSTANT DEMANDS THAT I GO TO THE TWENTY-FIRST CENTURY TO BRING HER BACK SOME STARBUCKS.
THERE'S ONLY SO MANY PEOPLE WHO WILL BUY THE LIE THAT I'M MAKING A SPIELBERG FILM, YOU KNOW?

SO WHAT'S YOUR PLAN?
I'LL MAKE SURE THAT ALL MY MEN ARE BY THE OAK OVER THERE BY TEN TOMORROW.
YOU BRING DOWN THE SHIELD AND FEED ON THE GIRL.
SINCE THE MANDRAKES WON'T WANT TO SHED THEIR SCALES AND FIGHT LIKE MEN, MORGEN WILL SEND US IN FIRST WITH THE ADONI.

BUT MY STONE LEGION WILL REACH YOU WELL AHEAD OF THE OTHER BONEHEADS. THAT'S WHEN YOU ZAP US OUT OF HERE.
YOU TRUST ME NOT TO LEAVE YOU BEHIND?
THREE DAYS AGO, I WOULDN'T HAVE TRUSTED YOU WITH $#@%.
BUT I'VE SEEN YOU WITH THAT WOMAN.
SHE TRUSTS YOU, SO I'M THINKING MAYBE SHE KNOWS SOMETHING I DON'T.

HEY GARAFYN.
WHAT ARE YOU GOING TO REPORT TO MORGEN?
THAT YOU'RE A $#@%HEAD WHO WOULDN'T LISTEN TO REASON.
NOW LOOK PISSED FOR THE BITCH.
I'LL SEE YA TOMORROW.

WELL?
I'M GOING TO DROP THE SHIELD TOMORROW BEFORE I'M COMPLETELY OUT OF POWER.
AND WHAT EXACTLY DO YOU PLAN TO DO WHEN THE SHIELD DROPS?

I'M GOING TO REGAIN MY STRENGTH AND GET US OUT OF HERE.
AND HOW DO YOU PROPOSE TO RECHARGE YOUR POWERS?

YOU'RE GOING TO KILL ME, AREN'T YOU?
NAY, SEREN! LIKE MORGEN AND LIKE ME, YOU ARE A MERLIN.
I KNEW THAT ALREADY WHEN I TOOK THE SPARK FROM YOU.
YOU ARE STRONG ENOUGH FOR ME TO—

WHAT NEW MADNESS IS THIS??!?
ME? A MERLIN? ARE YOU INSANE?
IT'S TRUE, SEREN. YOU ***ARE*** LIKE KERRIGAN AND MORGEN.
WELL, NOT COMPLETELY. FOR ONE, YOU'RE NOT EVIL.

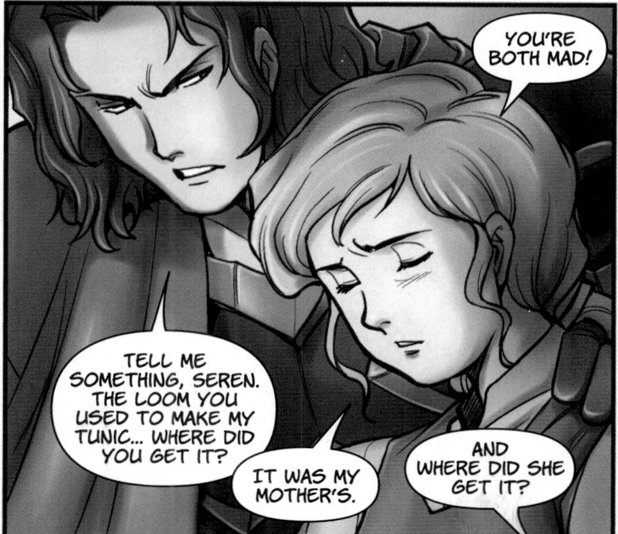
YOU'RE BOTH MAD!
TELL ME SOMETHING, SEREN. THE LOOM YOU USED TO MAKE MY TUNIC... WHERE DID YOU GET IT?
IT WAS MY MOTHER'S.
AND WHERE DID SHE GET IT?

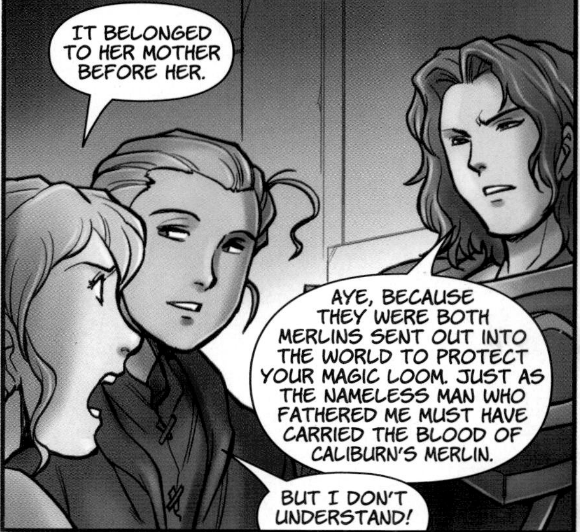
IT BELONGED TO HER MOTHER BEFORE HER.
AYE, BECAUSE THEY WERE BOTH MERLINS SENT OUT INTO THE WORLD TO PROTECT YOUR MAGIC LOOM. JUST AS THE NAMELESS MAN WHO FATHERED ME MUST HAVE CARRIED THE BLOOD OF CALIBURN'S MERLIN.
BUT I DON'T UNDERSTAND!

THEN I'LL SHOW YOU.

TRY TO STAB THE FABRIC YOU WOVE.
THIS IS RIDICULOUS. I'LL ONLY MAKE YOU ANGRY WHEN I CUT YOU.
NAY, I PROMISE. TRY TO STAB THE CLOTH.

THIS CAN'T BE! NOT A SINGLE THREAD HAS BEEN PRICKED BY THE DAGGER'S TIP, BUT I CUT THE CLOTH WITH SHEARS AND I STITCHED IT TOGETHER! WHY WON'T IT PART NOW?
NEITHER YOUR SHEARS NOR YOUR NEEDLE WERE WEAPONS OF WAR.

WHILE WEARING YOUR TUNIC, KERRIGAN CAN'T BE STABBED WITH A SWORD OR A DAGGER. BUT A PAIR OF SHEARS... DEADLY STUFF.
YOUR MOTHER'S LOOM IS THE LOOM OF CASWALLAN, ONE OF THE THIRTEEN SACRED OBJECTS GIVEN TO ARTHUR WHEN HE WAS CROWNED KING OF BRITAIN.
AFTER ARTHUR'S FALL, THE PENMERLIN RETURNED THE MAGICAL OBJECTS TO THE WAREMERLINS. THEY WERE INSTRUCTED TO HIDE THE OBJECTS FROM MORGEN, SINCE SHE WOULD HAVE USED THEIR POWER FOR EVIL.

EVER SINCE THAT DAY, MORGEN HAS BEEN SEARCHING FOR THE MISSING OBJECTS, AND FOR THOSE MERLINS WHO ARE BOUND TO PROTECT THEM.
IF I'M A MERLIN, WHY DON'T I HAVE ANY POWERS?
YOU DO.
YOUR MOTHER MUST HAVE BOUND THEM TO HIDE YOU FROM MORGEN AND TO PROTECT YOU FROM YOUR OWN DARKER SELF.
EVEN IN THE BEST PEOPLE A BATTLE RAGES BETWEEN GOOD AND EVIL, AND AS A MERLIN YOU MUST CHOOSE ONE OR THE OTHER.
I DO NOT WANT YOU TO HAVE TO FACE THAT CHOICE.

YOU ARE AFRAID I WOULD CHOOSE TO DESTROY... LIKE YOU DID.
BUT SEREN IS **GOOD**, SHE WOULD NEVER TURN TO THE DARK SIDE. IT IS NOT IN HER NATURE.
HUSH, BLAISE. LET HER BE.
NO MAN OR WOMAN KNOWS WHAT THEY WILL CHOOSE UNTIL THEY ARE FACED WITH THE CHOICE.

WHY DID YOU CHOOSE EVIL?
I HAD NO KNOWLEDGE OF GOODNESS OR OF DECENCY.
ALL MY LIFE I HAD BEEN SLAPPED AND SPAT ON AND ABUSED.
WHEN THE LORDS OF AVALON ASKED ME TO JOIN WITH THEM I THOUGHT THEY WERE LIKE THE ONES WHO HAD ALWAYS LOOKED DOWN UPON ME, SO I LAUGHED IN THEIR FACES.

I CHOSE MORGEN, FOR HER BEAUTY... AND HER POWER.
I DON'T WANT TO RUIN WHAT YOU ARE, SEREN.
BUT THE ONLY WAY I CAN UNLOCK YOUR MAGIC QUICKLY IS BY SHARING MY BLOOD WITH YOU, AND MY EVIL WILL CORRUPT YOU.
AND I SAY THAT YOU MUST GIVE ME THE CHANCE TO PROTECT MYSELF.
SINCE YOU CAN'T GIVE ME THE STRENGTH OF A WARRIOR, YOU CAN AT LEAST GIVE ME THE MAGIC OF A SORCERESS.
THEN THE DECISION IS MADE.
BLAISE, CAN YOU LEAVE US?
AYE, LORD KERRIGAN.

THE RED HAZE! I'M CHOKING!
BREATHE EASY, SEREN. THERE IS NOTHING TO FEAR.
THIS IS THE BLOOD CEREMONY, THAT WHICH WAS USED TO MARRY THE POWERS OF THE PENDRAGON WHO RULED THE PEOPLE TO THE PENMERLIN WHO COMMANDED THE ELEMENTS.
I AM USING IT TO MARRY MY POWERS TO YOURS.

AAAHH!

I'M SO SORRY, SEREN.

ENOUGH, SEREN!
IF YOU TAKE TOO MUCH YOU'LL KILL ME!

I WANT MORE!

AAAAHHH!
SHHH. LET THE POWER FLOW THROUGH YOU. DON'T LET IT CONSUME YOU!
OUR MINDS ARE JOINED AND OUR PASTS ARE ONE!

STOP, THIEF!
GET OUT OF MY SIGHT, WORM! YOU SICKEN ME. I SHOULD HAVE DROWNED YOU AT BIRTH!
HOW MUCH FOR AN HOUR WITH THE BOY?
HE'S A VIRGIN, MY LORD. SURELY THAT'S WORTH AT LEAST A SILVER MARK!
COME WITH ME, BOY, AND I WILL MAKE YOU A KING! I CAN GIVE YOU RICHES AND WOMEN AND POWER BEYOND YOUR IMAGINING. EVEN I WILL BE YOURS!
HE BELONGS TO US. MOVE AWAY FROM HIM, MORGEN, OR PERISH.
WE SERVE A HIGHER ORDER. CHASTITY, SACRIFICE, AND HUMILITY ARE OUR OATHS.
I'VE HAD ENOUGH OF CHASTITY, SACRIFICE, AND HUMILITY. I CHOOSE *POWER!*

I SAW...
I SAW WHAT THEY DID TO YOU.
AYE, LADY STAR. AS I SAW THE LOVE YOUR MOTHER GAVE YOU.

YOUR EYES... THEY USED TO BE BLUE.
THAT WAS A LONG TIME AGO.

TOMORROW WHEN I LOWER THE SHIELD I WILL HAVE TO FEED FROM YOU IMMEDIATELY.
IT WILL BE... PAINFUL.
BUT YOU MUSTN'T FIGHT ME, SEREN.
IF YOU TRY TO RUN AWAY I WON'T BE ABLE TO CONTROL THE HUNGER, AND THE FORCE OF MY FEEDING MAY KILL YOU.
DO YOU UNDERSTAND?
AYE, KERRIGAN. I WILL ENDURE WHATEVER PAIN YOU CAUSE.

LORD KERRIGAN, MAY I ENTER?
AYE, BLAISE.

SEREN, I WENT INTO YOUR ROOM TO CLEAR AWAY THE REMNANTS OF YOUR RED CLOTH, AND I FOUND THIS.
MY MOTHER'S STAR MEDALLION!
SHE GAVE IT TO ME IN A DREAM! I DIDN'T THINK IT WAS REAL!
IT IS A MERLIN'S MEDALLION, SEREN. AND PROVES THE TRUTH OF WHAT WE'VE TOLD YOU.
AYE.

AT TEN, GARAFYN AND THE OTHERS WILL BE WAITING BY THE EDGE OF THE SHIELD.
I WILL RAISE A DRAGON'S MIST AND LET THE SHIELD DROP.
ONCE I HAVE ENOUGH POWER, I'LL TRANSPORT US ALL TO THE TWENTY-FIRST CENTURY WHERE MORGEN'S ARMY WON'T BE ABLE TO FOLLOW US.

NOW WE MUST REST. TOMORROW WE WILL STAND TOGETHER AND WE WILL FIGHT MORGEN.
AYE, LORD KERRIGAN.
AYE, MY LORD. WE SHALL FIGHT MORGEN.
AND WE SHALL WIN.

The Next Day...
ARE YOU READY TO SURRENDER, KERRIGAN? YOU LOOK LIKE A CORPSE!
NAY, MORGEN! I WILL NEVER SURRENDER TO YOU!
IF I FALL, TAKE MY MEDALLION AND GET SEREN OUT OF HERE IMMEDIATELY!

OH DRAGON'S BREATH, THAT WHICH EMRYS PENMERLIN SUMMONED SO THAT UTHER PENDRAGON COULD LIE WITH IGRAINE AND SIRE KING ARTHUR, I CALL YOU NOW... RISE!
DRAGONS! HE'S RAISING THE MIST! DESCEND BEFORE IT BLINDS YOU!
GARGOYLES, PREPARE TO STORM THE SHIELD! THE MIST WILL DRAIN THE LAST OF KERRIGAN'S POWERS AND THE SHIELD WILL DROP!
ADONI, READY YOUR ARROWS!

THE NATURAL-BORN GARGOYLES ARE TOO LUMBERING TO MOVE QUICKLY IN THIS MIST, AND MORGEN WON'T RISK STRIKING SEREN WITH ONE OF THE ADONI'S ARROWS DESPITE HER THREATS. THE CHILD IS TOO PRECIOUS.
THE TIME IS NOW! I MUST LET THE SHIELD DROP AND FEED!
IT WILL HURT, SEREN, BUT LIKE KERRIGAN SAID, YOU MUSTN'T FIGHT IT!

AAAAHHH!

I CAN'T! I CAN'T GO THROUGH WITH IT!
BUT YOU MUST, LORD! YOU MUST REGAIN YOUR STRENGTH!
NAY, SEREN! NOT AT THE COST OF YOUR LIFE!
THEN I GUESS WE'D BETTER PREPARE TO FIGHT OUR WAY OUT!

RUN, MEN! RUN TOWARDS KERRIGAN! WE'RE ABOUT TO SHAKE THIS $#@%-HOLE AND BOOGIE INTO THE TWENTY-FIRST CENTURY!

TRAITORS!
KILL THEM!

RUN!

LET'S GO!
WE'VE FOUND A SMALL SNAG...
I CAN'T FEED FROM SEREN!
BULL$#@%!
YOU'VE BEEN FEEDING FROM PEOPLE FOR WHAT, SIX HUNDRED YEARS OR SOMETHING?
NOW GROW A BALL AND SUCK THE JUICE FROM YOUR PET HERE BEFORE MORGEN SMASHES US ALL AND MAKES US INTO A DRIVEWAY!

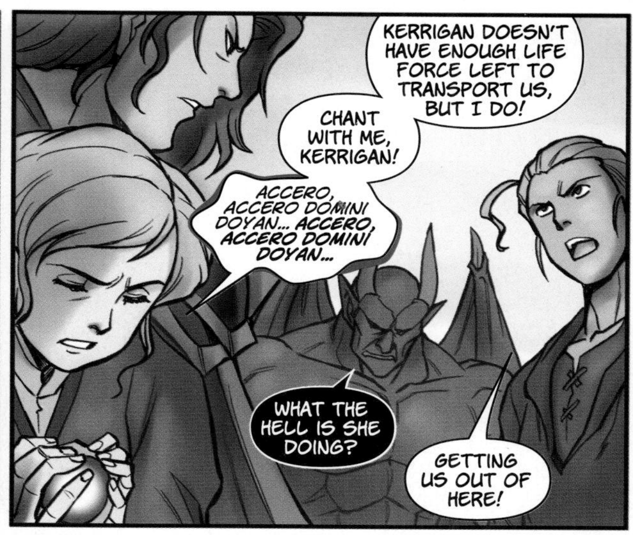
KERRIGAN DOESN'T HAVE ENOUGH LIFE FORCE LEFT TO TRANSPORT US, BUT I DO!
CHANT WITH ME, KERRIGAN!
ACCERO, ACCERO DOMINI DOYAN... ACCERO, ACCERO DOMINI DOYAN...
WHAT THE HELL IS SHE DOING?
GETTING US OUT OF HERE!

ACCERO, ACCERO DOMINI DOYAN...

KABLAM!

THUMP!

WHAT IS THAT?
DOES MORGEN SEND ARMORED DRAGONS AGAINST US?
IT'S A PLANE.
A WHAT?
BIG. SILVER. BIRD.
PEOPLE CLIMB INTO IT AND FLY FROM ONE PLACE TO ANOTHER.

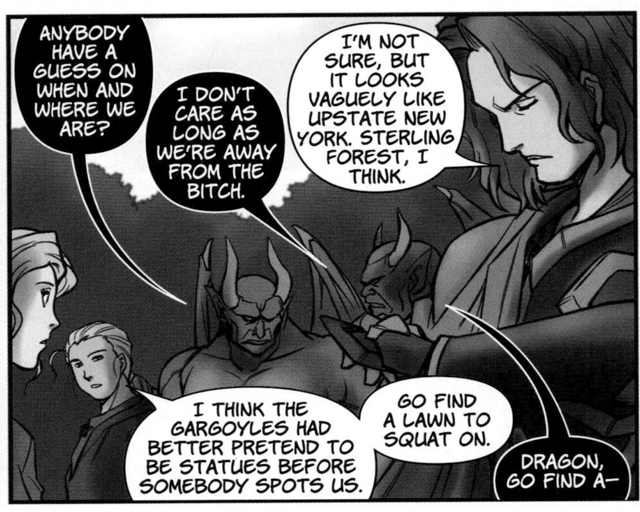
ANYBODY HAVE A GUESS ON WHEN AND WHERE WE ARE?
I DON'T CARE AS LONG AS WE'RE AWAY FROM THE BITCH.
I'M NOT SURE, BUT IT LOOKS VAGUELY LIKE UPSTATE NEW YORK. STERLING FOREST, I THINK.
I THINK THE GARGOYLES HAD BETTER PRETEND TO BE STATUES BEFORE SOMEBODY SPOTS US.
GO FIND A LAWN TO SQUAT ON.
DRAGON, GO FIND A–

ENOUGH!
BLAISE IS RIGHT. TOGETHER WE ARE TOO CONSPICUOUS AND WE ARE A MAGNET FOR MORGEN'S ADONI.
YEA, WELL, I'M NOT GOING TO GO AND PRETEND TO BE A LAWN ORNAMENT, NO MATTER WHAT THE DRAGON SAYS.
WHAT'S A LAWN ORNAMENT?
A STATUE THAT SITS IN A YARD WHERE DOGS PISS ALL OVER IT.

WELL, FEEL FREE TO RETURN TO CAMELOT ANY TIME YOU WANT.
YEAH RIGHT. AFTER WE'VE JUST SCREWED QUEEN BITCH?
WATCH OUT!

GOTCHA!

NO!

KRAK!

WHY DID YOU DO THAT?
I THOUGHT I WAS HELPING!
I COULD HAVE FED ON HIM!

LET GO!

DROP HER OR DIE!

I SAID, LET HER GO!
GOOD TO THE LAST DROP, HUH?
DON'T START WITH ME, GARAFYN.
I'M NOW STRONG ENOUGH TO PULL YOUR WINGS OFF YOUR BACK AND LAUGH WHILE I DO IT.
POINT WELL TAKEN.
BUT I THINK IT'S TIME TO PUT MY POWERS TO A BETTER USE.
ACCERO, ACCERO DOMINI DOYAN . .
WHAT'S HE DOING?
CREATING A TEMPORARY SCRAMBLER.
IT WILL KEEP THE REST OF MORGEN'S FORCES FROM PINPOINTING OUR LOCATION, AT LEAST FOR A LITTLE WHILE.
BUT IT'S ONLY A MATTER OF TIME BEFORE MORE FIND US, ISN'T IT?
AYE, SEREN.
THEN WHAT ARE WE GOING TO DO?
MOST LIKELY BLEED... A LOT.

IT WOULD BE EASIER TO HIDE IF YOU TWO SPLIT UP.
THE POWER OF THREE MERLINS IS PRETTY DAMNED HARD TO MISS.
I WON'T LEAVE HER UNPROTECTED.
YEAH? WELL IF WE DON'T HIDE, MORGEN WILL TURN YOU AND SEREN INTO A FILLET AS SOON AS THE BABY CAN BREATHE ON ITS OWN.
WHO PLANNED THIS ESCAPE ANYWAY?
THAT WOULD BE THE TWO WHO HAVE ROCKS FOR BRAINS.
I RESENT THAT! IT'S TRUE, BUT I STILL RESENT IT.
I HATE TO SAY IT, BUT GARAFYN IS RIGHT. WE NEED TO SPLIT UP.

ANIR, GARAFYN, HERE'S PAYMENT FOR SERVICES RENDERED.
WITH THIS; YOU'LL BE ABLE TO TRAVEL THROUGH TIME, AND HIDE FROM MORGEN.
YOU MEAN YOU'RE NOT GOING TO TRY TO ENSLAVE US, LIKE MORGEN DID?

THERE'S BEEN ENOUGH SLAVERY. YOU'RE FREE.

THANKS, KERRIGAN. MAYBE SOMEDAY WE'LL BE ABLE TO RETURN THE FAVOR.
YOU ALREADY HAVE.

PHZZ!

THAT WAS VERY KIND.
IT WAS NECESSARY. GARAFYN WAS RIGHT. WE HAVE TO SEPARATE.
ALL OF US.

BREA!
BREA OF THE TUATHA DÉ DANANN! IF YOU WANT YOUR SWORD BACK, COME AND TAKE IT!

WHY HAVE YOU SUMMONED ME?
I WANT YOU TO TAKE SEREN TO AVALON.
I WON'T GO WITH HIM!
BACK IN JOYOUS GARD, HE PRETENDED TO BE LANCELOT.
HE CALLED YOU A DEMON AND TRIED TO MAKE ME STEAL YOUR SWORD!

I'LL JOIN YOU IN AVALON.
BUT KERRIGAN...
WE'LL TALK ABOUT IT LATER, BLAISE.
WHY WON'T *YOU* TAKE ME?
I CAN'T. YOU'LL NEED AN ESCORT THROUGH THE VEIL, AND I GAVE MY KEY TO THE GARGOYLES.

BUT I HAVE MY MEDALLION.
YOU'LL STILL NEED BREA TO MAKE THE INTRODUCTIONS FOR YOU AT AVALON AND TO MAKE SURE THAT NOTHING HAPPENS TO YOU.
BUT WHY AREN'T YOU COMING?
I NEED TO FETCH YOUR LOOM BEFORE MORGEN FINDS IT... IF SHE HASN'T ALREADY.

KERRIGAN, YOU CAN'T...
I SAID WE'LL DISCUSS IT LATER, BLAISE.
WILL YOU WATCH SEREN? I NEED TO HAVE A WORD ALONE WITH BREA.

I'LL BE RIGHT BACK.
YOU'D BEST BE, MY LORD.

YOU SAID SOMETHING ABOUT THE SWORD?
AYE. IF YOU PROMISE TO PERSONALLY PROTECT SEREN, I'LL GIVE YOU THE SWORD IN TRADE.
THERE'S A "BUT" IN THERE, I SENSE IT.
I WANT YOUR WORD THAT WHEN MY CHILD IS OLD ENOUGH, THE SWORD WILL BE PASSED TO HIM.

THAT'S IT?
YOU WILL TRUST MY WORD?
IF YOU SWEAR BY THE GODDESS DANU, AYE.
WHAT HAS CHANGED ABOUT YOU?

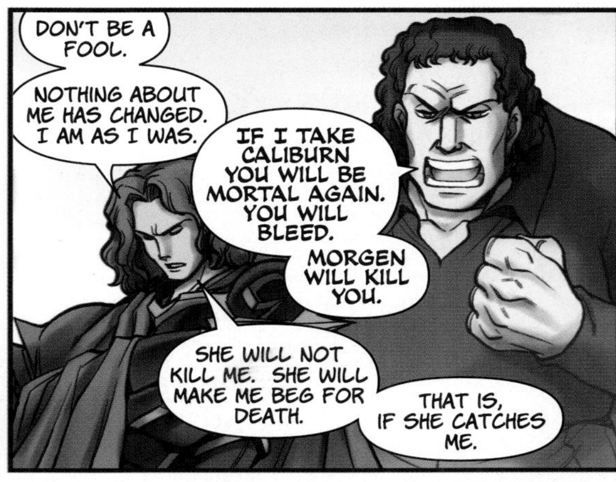
DON'T BE A FOOL.
NOTHING ABOUT ME HAS CHANGED. I AM AS I WAS.
IF I TAKE CALIBURN YOU WILL BE MORTAL AGAIN. YOU WILL BLEED.
MORGEN WILL KILL YOU.
SHE WILL NOT KILL ME. SHE WILL MAKE ME BEG FOR DEATH.
THAT IS, IF SHE CATCHES ME.

GIVE ME YOUR WORD THAT YOU WILL TAKE SEREN TO AVALON AND THAT YOU WILL PROTECT HER AND HER BABY.
YOU HAVE MY WORD.
ON THE BLOOD OF DANU?
ON THE BLOOD OF DANU.

NOW GIVE ME THE SWORD.
NOT YET.

YOU MEAN TO CHEAT ME, DEMON?
NAY! BUT IF I GIVE THE SWORD TO YOU NOW, SEREN WILL KNOW SOMETHING IS AMISS AND SHE WILL NEVER GO WITH YOU TO AVALON!

WISELY REASONED.

BUT EASILY DEALT WITH,

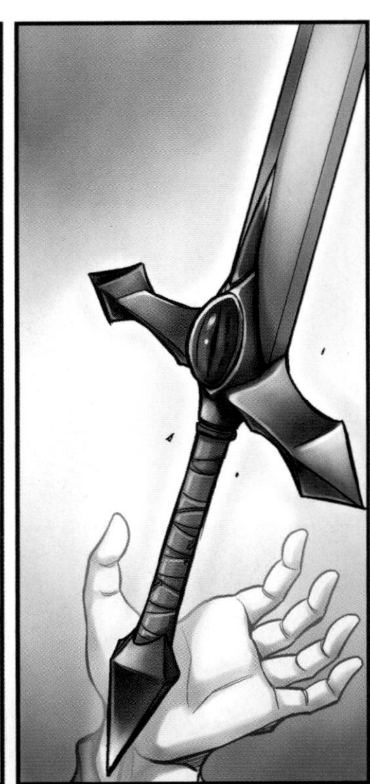

HERE.
IT HAS NO POWERS, BUT SHE WON'T KNOW THAT UNLESS SHE TOUCHES IT.

NAY, LORD KERRIGAN! THIS IS A TRAP!
FOR CENTURIES WE HAVE BEEN TOGETHER! I AM YOURS... WE BELONG TO EACH OTHER!
I DON'T WANT TO BUT I MUST!

YOU REALLY LET GO OF IT!
THE SEPARATION... IT BURNS!
SEREN IS NOT TO KNOW OF THIS UNTIL SHE IS SAFELY IN AVALON!

And Soon...
YOU MUST GO WITH BREA NOW.
BLAISE WILL ACCOMPANY YOU.
NAY, I WOULD RATHER HE GO WITH YOU TO FETCH THE LOOM.
BUT...
NAY KERRIGAN. DON'T ARGUE. YOU MAY NEED BLAISE'S HELP.
AYE MY LORD. THERE IS TREACHERY EVERYWHERE.
WE MUST GO... AND SOON.

YOU WILL BE CAREFUL?
AYE.
I WILL COUNT THE MOMENTS UNTIL YOU RETURN TO ME.
AS WILL I.

YOU MUST GO NOW, SEREN.

...

I WILL SEE YOU ANON.

KERRIGAN, I HAVE AN AWFUL FEELING...

KERRIGAN! BEHIND YOU!
FLASH!

KERRIGAN!

PHZZ!

DAMN MORGEN AND HER PERSISTENCE.

SO HOW ARE YOU GOING TO GET SEREN BACK? YOU'LL NEVER GET ARTHUR'S TABLE WITHOUT HER.
WHY DO I NEED A TABLE? I CAN'T EVEN EAT!
HELLO? WHAT ABOUT WEALTH, POWER, WORLD DOMINATION?
DID THAT ADONI KNOCK SOMETHING LOOSE IN YOUR HEAD?

MORE?
ISN'T THAT BITCH MORGEN EVER GOING TO LAY OFF!?!
FLASSH!

WHUD!

HEY, WATCH IT!
OOF!

KLANGG!

OOOFF!

DIE, DAMN YOU!
SHUK!

AAH!
SLASH!

THE KERRIGAN BLEEDS?

PHZZ!
WE NEED TO GET OUT OF HERE BEFORE THE ADONI RETURN WITH REINFORCEMENTS.

EVEN NOW THEY'RE REPORTING TO MORGEN THAT I HAVE BEEN WOUNDED.
HOW COULD YOU GIVE CALIBURN TO BREA?
MORGEN WILL--
BELIEVE ME, I KNOW.

WE NEED TO GET THAT LOOM BEFORE MORGEN FINDS IT.
AYE.
SO HOW ARE WE GOING TO GET THERE?

SEREN'S MAGIC.

At that Same Time...
IS THIS AVALON?
AYE.
IT LOOKS LIKE HEAVEN.
NOT ENTIRELY. NOTHING IS EVER PERFECT, BUT THIS COMES CLOSE. YOU WILL BE HAPPY HERE.

COME, CHILD. THERE ARE MANY PEOPLE WHO WISH TO MEET YOU.

BREA, I SEE YOU FOUND OUR WAYWARD STEWARD.
NOT EXACTLY, RATHER, SHE FOUND ME.
AQUILA PENMERLIN, MEET SEREN.
SEREN, MEET AQUILA PENMERLIN.

CALL ME MERLIN, SEREN. MOST PEOPLE DO.

BREA, YOU HAVE BROUGHT CALIBURN TO AVALON?
NAY. CALIBURN IS WITH KERRIGAN, ISN'T IT? I SAW IT STRAPPED TO HIS HIPS!

KERRIGAN GAVE IT TO ME IN EXCHANGE FOR MY BRINGING YOU HERE.

HE WANTED TO MAKE SURE THAT THE SWORD WENT TO YOUR CHILD, SO I AM FULFILLING MY PART OF THE BARGAIN.
I CAN'T BELIEVE THAT HE RELINQUISHED IT.
I CAN.
HE DID IT FOR ME.
AND WHEN I FIND HIM, I'M GOING TO KILL HIM FOR BEING SO STUPID!

Seren's Former Lodgings...
ALL OF SEREN'S BELONGINGS ARE IN THIS TRUNK, MY LORD.
WHO ARE YOU, GIRL?
WENDLYN, MY LORD.
WENDLYN... YOU WERE SEREN'S FRIEND.
AYE, MY LORD. I WAS.

THIS WAS ALL SHE OWNED?
YES, MY LORD.

WHAT'S THIS?
THE HERALDIC DRAGON OF AVALON...ARTHUR'S SYMBOL.

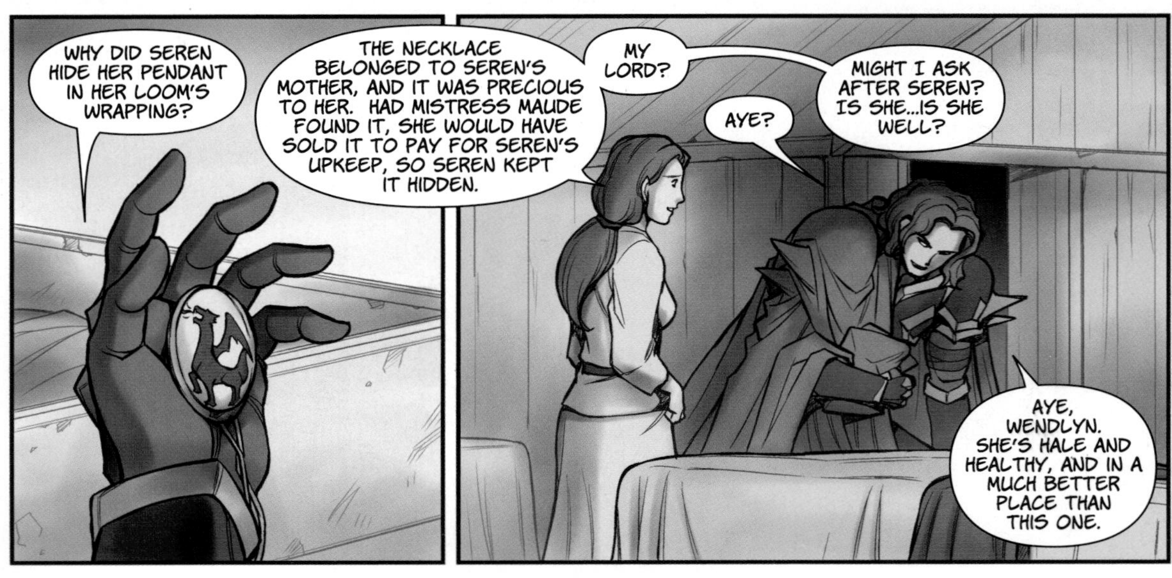
WHY DID SEREN HIDE HER PENDANT IN HER LOOM'S WRAPPING?
THE NECKLACE BELONGED TO SEREN'S MOTHER, AND IT WAS PRECIOUS TO HER. HAD MISTRESS MAUDE FOUND IT, SHE WOULD HAVE SOLD IT TO PAY FOR SEREN'S UPKEEP, SO SEREN KEPT IT HIDDEN.
MY LORD?
AYE?
MIGHT I ASK AFTER SEREN? IS SHE...IS SHE WELL?
AYE, WENDLYN. SHE'S HALE AND HEALTHY, AND IN A MUCH BETTER PLACE THAN THIS ONE.

YOU'RE NOT EVEN GOING TO *ATTEMPT* TO JOIN SEREN IN AVALON, ARE YOU?
NAY.
THE LORDS OF AVALON WOULD NEVER ALLOW ME TO SET FOOT ON THEIR SHORES.
WE HAVE BEEN AT WAR FAR TOO LONG FOR THEM TO WELCOME MY PRESENCE.
PLINK!

HONESTLY, I DON'T WANT TO GO TO AVALON EITHER. YOU KNOW HOW I FEEL ABOUT GOOD GUYS.
THEY'RE BORING.
MORGEN WILL KILL YOU IF YOU STAY WITH ME.
BESIDES, SEREN WILL BE LONELY AND AFRAID THERE. SHE'LL NEED A FRIEND.
SHE WOULD RATHER HAVE YOU.
DO YOU WISH ME TO PASS ON A MESSAGE TO SEREN?

WORDS ARE EVER DECEITFUL.
THERE IS NOTHING MORE TO BE SAID BETWEEN US.

IT HAS BEEN AN HONOR TO BE WITH YOU ALL THESE CENTURIES, KERRIGAN.
I'VE ALWAYS CONSIDERED YOU A FRIEND.
I KNOW.
THAT'S WHY I NEVER KILLED YOU FOR YOUR INSUBORDINATION.

WAIT, BLAISE. I WOULD ASK ONE MORE FAVOR OF YOU.
AND THAT IS?
FIND SOMEONE TO MARRY SEREN BEFORE SHE SHOWS HER PREGNANCY.
SHE DOES NOT WANT HER CHILD TO BE BORN A BASTARD.
AND IF SHE'S UNWILLING?
SHE WON'T BE.

GOD SPEED YOU, KERRIGAN.
GOD SPEED *YOU*, MY FRIEND.
HE WAS NEVER WITH THE LIKES OF ME.
PHZZ!

FOR THE WOMAN I LOVE, IT IS TIME TO FINISH THIS.
EVEN WITHOUT SEREN'S NECKLACE AND WITHOUT MY SWORD, I COULD STILL TIME-TRAVEL.

BUT TO WHAT PURPOSE?
THERE IS ONLY ONE WAY TO MAKE SURE THAT NONE OF MY KIND EVER HUNTS SEREN AGAIN.
MORGEN!
IF YOU WANT ME, I'M HERE!

FLASSH!
WHERE IS SHE?
SHE'S GONE.
GONE WHERE?
AVALON.

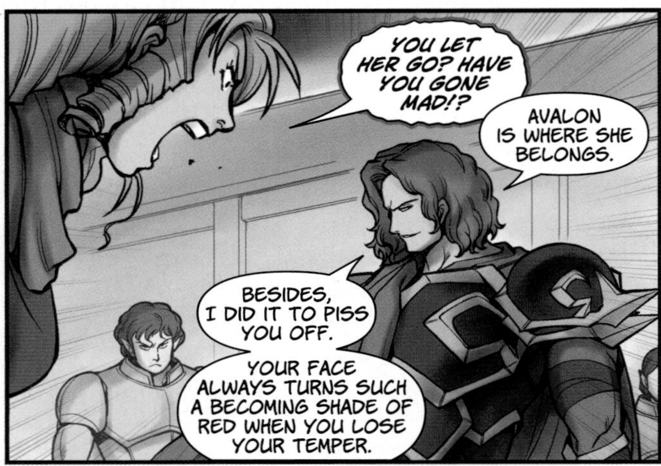
YOU LET HER GO? HAVE YOU GONE MAD!?
AVALON IS WHERE SHE BELONGS.
BESIDES, I DID IT TO PISS YOU OFF.
YOUR FACE ALWAYS TURNS SUCH A BECOMING SHADE OF RED WHEN YOU LOSE YOUR TEMPER.

I MAY HAVE LOST MY TEMPER AND MY PAWN, BUT YOU, DEAR BOY...

YOU ARE GOING TO LOSE MORE THAN THAT. A *LOT* MORE!

Avalon

SEREN! PUT THE SWORD DOWN!

NAY! WITH THIS SWORD IN MY HANDS, NO ONE CAN HURT ME OR MY BABY!

NO ONE IS GOING TO HURT YOU HERE, SEREN!

YOUR BODY IS TRYING TO ACCLIMATIZE ITSELF TO THE EVIL THAT KERRIGAN GAVE YOU.

FORCE YOUR ***OWN*** WILL INTO YOUR HAND AND DROP THE SWORD; THEN I WILL BRING YOU A PURGE TO REMOVE HIS POWERS FROM YOU!

NAY! I DON'T WANT A PURGE!

I WANT TO KEEP KERRIGAN WITHIN ME!

FLASH!
SEREN!

STOP THIS!
BLAISE?
NAY! I WANT THE POWER. IT NOURISHES ME!
BUT IT COULD KILL YOUR BABY.
THIS DARK POWER IS KERRIGAN'S TO WIELD, NOT YOURS.
LET IT GO.

WHERE IS KERRIGAN?
I LEFT HIM IN LONDON.

LET GO OF ME! YOU PROMISED TO BRING KERRIGAN!
I KNOW, SEREN. I KNOW.
AND YOU HAVE THE MEDALLION! HE'LL NEVER REACH US NOW!
TRY TO UNDERSTAND, SEREN. IT'S FOR THE BEST.
KERRIGAN DOESN'T BELONG HERE.

THEN BLAISE AND I DON'T BELONG HERE EITHER!
YES YOU DO!
BLAISE HAS BEEN OUR SECRET FRIEND AND CONFIDANT FOR A VERY LONG TIME. AND YOU ARE THE MOTHER OF THE NEXT PENMERLIN!

BUT SOMEONE MUST RESCUE KERRIGAN! ONCE MORGEN REALIZES THAT HE IS NO LONGER PROTECTED BY HIS SWORD, SHE WILL KILL HIM!
WE CANNOT VOLUNTARILY ENTER MORGEN'S DOMAIN. IF WE DO, SHE WILL HAVE THE POWER TO DESTROY THE ENTIRE WORLD.
I DON'T CARE! GIVE ME SOME OF YOUR KNIGHTS.
SO YOU CAN DO WHAT? STORM THE CASTLE? FIGHT A THOUSAND GARGOYLES AND DRAGONS?

THEN WHAT WOULD YOU HAVE ME DO?
I WOULD HAVE YOU DO WHAT KERRIGAN WANTED.
AND WHAT YOU SHOULD HAVE DONE FROM THE BEGINNING! MARRY ONE OF OUR KNIGHTS AND RAISE YOUR CHILD!

I'D RATHER RESCUE KERRIGAN ALONE.

AREN'T YOU GOING TO STOP HER?
BUT IF MORGEN CAPTURES HER, WE LOSE EVERYTHING! SHE GAMBLES WITH ALL OF OUR FATES!
I CAN'T STOP HER. SHE HAS THE POWER OF TWO MERLINS AND THE RESOLVE OF A WOMAN WHO WANTS TO PROTECT WHAT SHE LOVES.
WHO KNOWS? PERHAPS SHE WILL SUCCEED. AFTER ALL, SHE RETURNED CALIBURN TO US, AND SHE HAS TURNED KERRIGAN AWAY FROM THE EVIL HE HAS SERVED FOR CENTURIES.
IT WAS KERRIGAN'S CHOICE TO SERVE MORGEN!
YES. BUT IT WAS ALSO KERRIGAN'S CHOICE TO SACRIFICE HIMSELF TO ASSURE SEREN'S SAFETY. HE HAS CHANGED, AGRAVAIN. I FEEL IT IN MY BONES.

Camelot
POOR WORM! LOOK AT YOU. YESTERDAY YOU WERE KING OF CAMELOT. NOW YOU ARE NOTHING BUT A NAMELESS SLAVE. WORTHLESS! AND FOR WHAT?
KRAK!

FOR A PEASANT WHO CARES NOTHING FOR YOU!
FOR A LITTLE WHORE!

SHE'S NOT A WHORE!
CRACK!

YOU PATHETIC OAF. I CAN'T BELIEVE I EVER TOOK SOMETHING AS WORTHLESS AS YOU INTO MY BED.

YOU CALLED FOR ME, MY QUEEN?
DRAG THIS WRETCH INTO THE HALL. I HAVE SOMETHING FUN PLANNED FOR HIM.

GOOD ADONI, MANDRAKES, AND KNIGHTS OF MY TABLE.
'TIS TIME TO CROWN THE NEXT KING OF CAMELOT.

TELL ME, WHO AMONG YOU HAS THE COURAGE TO BATTLE KERRIGAN NOW?

THE KING WILL SOON BE DEAD.
LONG LIVE THE NEW ONE.

MASDEN? CARE TO BE THE ONCE AND FUTURE KING?

GET UP AND FIGHT, YOU WORTHLESS DOG!

LOOK, THE SLAVE IS TRYING TO BE KINGLY.
BUT ONCE RUBBISH, ALWAYS RUBBISH.
TO HELL WITH YOU, MORGEN!

HA!
KILL HIM, MASDEN!

CLANG!

SEREN!
OH, THIS IS RICH!
LOOK WHAT HAS RETURNED OF HER OWN FREE WILL TO OUR COMPANY!
BIG MISTAKE, LITTLE GIRL! BIG MISTAKE!

LET GO OF HIM, YOU BITCH!
YOU WANT HIM, WHORE?
THEN YOU CAN HAVE HIM...

DEAD!
NAY!

ATIERA GARA TUAWAHA ETHRA VERUS TIERA!
ATIERA GARA TUAWAHA ETHRA VERUS TIERA!
SEREN! STOP!
THWACK!

IN THE WHISPER OF THE ANCIENT STONE AND IN THE MIST THAT BELONGS TO THE DRAGONS, MY BREATH IS YOUR BREATH.

MY HEART IS YOUR HEART AND MY LIFE IS YOUR LIFE!

NAY!
YOU MUST LIVE!
ATIERA GARA TUAWAHA ETHRA VERUS TIERA!

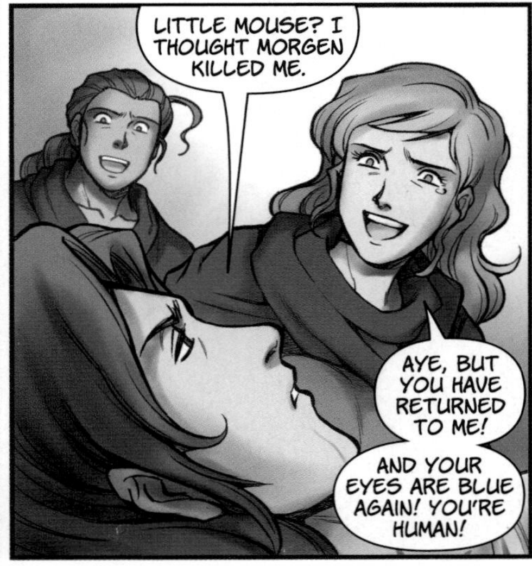
LITTLE MOUSE? I THOUGHT MORGEN KILLED ME.
AYE, BUT YOU HAVE RETURNED TO ME!
AND YOUR EYES ARE BLUE AGAIN! YOU'RE HUMAN!

FOOLS! DO YOU REALLY THINK YOU CAN COMPETE WITH ME?
YOU CAN'T DEFEAT US MORGEN!
OH, BUT I CAN! JUST TRY USING YOUR MAGIC TO LEAVE HERE!
THE MINUTE YOU DROP YOUR GUARD, I'LL BLAST YOU!

LIKE THIS!
HOW DO WE END THIS?
WE END THIS WHEN YOU DROP THAT BRAT. THEN I WILL HAVE THE POWER TO KILL YOU BOTH!

SKRASSH

GET OFF ME, YOU OAFS! WHAT DO YOU THINK YOU'RE DOING?
PROTECTING YOU, MY QUEEN!
WHATEVER YOU DO, LEGION, DON'T LET THE EVIL LORDS OF AVALON BLAST MORGEN!

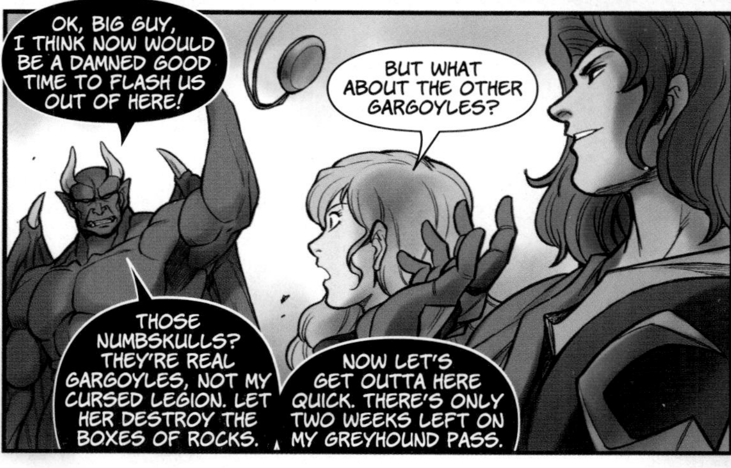
OK, BIG GUY, I THINK NOW WOULD BE A DAMNED GOOD TIME TO FLASH US OUT OF HERE!
BUT WHAT ABOUT THE OTHER GARGOYLES?
THOSE NUMBSKULLS? THEY'RE REAL GARGOYLES, NOT MY CURSED LEGION. LET HER DESTROY THE BOXES OF ROCKS.
NOW LET'S GET OUTTA HERE QUICK. THERE'S ONLY TWO WEEKS LEFT ON MY GREYHOUND PASS.

Avalon
WHAT IS THE MEANING OF THIS?
KERRIGAN IS A THREAT TO ALL OF US.
AND YOU CALL YOURSELF A FRIEND OF AVALON?
YES? AND SO IS YOUR INCOMPETENT BROTHER AGRAVAIN, YET YOU LET HIM LIVE...AND IN THE CASTLE, NO LESS!
FLASSH!

I HAVE SEEN HOW MUCH KERRIGAN HAS SUFFERED TO PROTECT SEREN!
IF YOU THROW HIM OUT, THEN I GO WITH HIM!
AS DO I.
LIKE I HAVE ANY CHOICE, HUH?
THIS IS TREASON! WAIT UNTIL I TELL MERLIN! WAIT...

WELCOME HOME, KERRIGAN.
HUH??
IS THIS A TRICK?
NAY. I WOULD NEVER PLAY WITH ANYONE SO CRUELLY. I AM NOT MORGEN.
MERLIN, YOU'RE NOT JUST GOING TO FORGIVE HIM FOR ALL HE'S DONE! ARE YOU?

WE'VE ALL MADE MISTAKES, HAVEN'T WE, GAWAIN?
AND IF I REMEMBER CORRECTLY, YOU AND YOUR BROTHER WERE THE CAUSE OF THIS TROUBLE IN THE FIRST PLACE.
ALL RIGHT MERLIN. IF YOU INSIST. BUT I STILL DON'T TRUST THE DEMON, AND I'LL BE WATCHING HIM.

WELCOME TO AVALON, KERRIGAN.
I'M SURE SEREN WILL BE MOST DELIGHTED TO SHOW YOU TO YOUR ROOMS.
ABSOLUTELY.

YOU, EVIL MAN, MADE ME A PROMISE THAT YOU HAVE YET TO FULFILL.
AND THAT IS?
TO GIVE MY BABY A NAME.
THAT IS ONE PROMISE I FULLY INTEND TO KEEP.
GOOD, BECAUSE I WANT TO MAKE AN HONEST MAN OF YOU.
I WOULDN'T GO QUITE THAT FAR, LADY MOUSE. THERE'S ONLY SO MUCH CHANGING A MAN CAN DO.
HRMPH...

WE SHALL SEE, MY LORD. WE SHALL SEE.
OUCH!

And so, as in all good fairy tales, Seren and Kerrigan live happily ever after.

But the war between Avalon and Camelot ...

...is far from over.

(issue 1 variant cover by Tom Grummett, Terry Pallot and Guru eFX)